"Hazel Conley and Margaret Page's book offers an important and thought-provoking study of equality law in practice, and of feminist encounters with the local state as decision-maker, service provider and employer. Conley and Page's clear-sighted yet impassioned account of how equality practitioners engage with the law, in particular with the short-lived but ground breaking 'gender equality duty', is of particular interest for lawyers seeking examples of 'reflexive legislation' in action. It deserves to be an important part of the legal, as well as policy, debates on equality."

Diamond Ashiagbor, *Professor of Law,*
SOAS University of London, UK

"*Gender Equality in Public Services* should be essential reading for all gender equality practitioners in local authorities in England and women's equality activists more generally. It is rigorous and readable, original and timely."

Judith Squires, *Professor, University of Bristol, UK*

"Informed by feminist theory, Page and Conley provide a comprehensive review of feminist engagement with the proactive, liberating and coercive welfare state at the macro level, before delivering a thoughtful account of the implementation of the gender equality duty within the local state. Emphasising gender equality as a 'direction of travel' rather than a 'single destination', the book elaborates the tensions which beset the search for gender equality, whilst profiling the fundamental institutional work enacted by activists and equality officers on the ground. This is an important text for those researching, studying and performing equality."

Dr. Rachel Ashworth, *Reader in Public Services*
Management, Cardiff University, UK

T0298378

Gender Equality in Public Services

The provision of state funded and democratically accountable care services represents one of the most potentially transformative advances in gendered social relations and equality for women by 'defamilising' care and providing paid work. But the cost of providing these services, which women have access to them and how they should be provided are always at the forefront of debate, especially during economic crises. Socially funded and publicly accountable care services are therefore a key site of feminist activity, but also the frontline for spending cuts and 'reform' during times of austerity.

Gender Equality in Public Services analyses how gender equality work in British public services is changing in response to factors including: equality legislation; the erosion of local democracy; privatisation of public services; and new forms of feminist activism and leadership. It also assesses the challenges and opportunities for promoting women's equality in producing and using public services.

Impacting upon developed and developing economies, the arguments in this challenging book explore the potential of equality and feminist activism and leadership for radical and transformational change. It will appeal to advanced students, researchers and practitioners interested in social policy, feminist organisation theory, equal opportunities and gender mainstreaming practice.

Hazel Conley is Reader in Human Resource Management in the Centre for Research in Equality and Diversity at Queen Mary University of London. She is the joint editor of *The Gower Handbook of Discrimination at Work*.

Margaret Page is a Senior Lecturer in organisation studies in Bristol Business School, University of the West of England, UK. Her research and teaching investigates the practices and organization of gender equality and supports managers and activists who promote women's equality and diversity in public services.

Routledge studies in management, organizations and society

This series presents innovative work grounded in new realities, addressing issues crucial to an understanding of the contemporary world. This is the world of organised societies, where boundaries between formal and informal, public and private, local and global organizations have been displaced or have vanished, along with other nineteenth century dichotomies and oppositions. Management, apart from becoming a specialized profession for a growing number of people, is an everyday activity for most members of modern societies.

Similarly, at the level of enquiry, culture and technology, and literature and economics, can no longer be conceived as isolated intellectual fields; conventional canons and established mainstreams are contested. **Management, Organizations and Society** addresses these contemporary dynamics of transformation in a manner that transcends disciplinary boundaries, with books that will appeal to researchers, student and practitioners alike.

Other titles in this series:

Gender Equality in Public Services

Chasing the dream

Hazel Conley and Margaret Page

Routledge
Taylor & Francis Group

LONDON AND NEW YORK

First published 2015
by Routledge
2 Park Square, Milton Park, Abingdon, Oxon OX14 4RN

and by Routledge
605 Third Avenue, New York, NY 10017

First issued in paperback 2020

Routledge is an imprint of the Taylor & Francis Group, an informa business

British Library Cataloguing in Publication Data
A catalogue record for this book is available from the British Library

Library of Congress Cataloging-in-Publication Data
A catalog record for this book has been requested

ISBN 13: 978-0-367-73908-9 (pbk)
ISBN 13: 978-0-415-62776-4 (hbk)

Typeset in Sabon
by Taylor & Francis Books

The whole [of] equalities work is like that really. Running around with a butterfly net!

Equality advisor, local government

This book is dedicated to practitioners and activists who campaign to protect and to extend the long agenda for women's equality within local, democratically accountable public services. Without your efforts, things would be much worse.

Contents

Case studies

Boxes

Acknowledgements

This book has its roots in our research with gender equality practitioners and women's equality activists in local authorities in England. We would like to thank all those who contributed to our case studies of implementation of the Gender Equality Duty in local authorities, and those who contributed to our inquiry into the politics of local authority women's and gender equality work in its earlier phases.

In particular we thank the following for their encouragement, practical suggestions and time in contributing to the development of this project:

Diane Banyon, Helen Brown, Sue Durbin, Jane Grant, Sue Ledwith, Di Parkin, Helen Scadding, Marion Scott, Josephine Zara.

We would also like to thank the British Academy, who funded our research, The University of the West of England, Bristol and Queen Mary University of London for allowing sabbatical time for writing the book, and Stella Warren for assisting with preparation of the manuscript.

Abbreviations

BTF	Beyond the Fragments
CCT	Compulsory Competitive Tendering
CEB	Corporate Equalities Board
CEDAW	Committee on the Elimination of Discrimination Against Women
CMB	Corporate Management Board
CRE	Commission for Racial Equality
CSW	Commission on the Status of Women
DLR	Discrimination Law Review
DRC	Disability Rights Commission
EHRC	Equalities and Human Rights Commission
EIA	Equality Impact Assessment
EOC	Equal Opportunities Commission
EU	European Union
GDP	Gross Domestic Product
GED	Gender Equality Duty
GEO	Government Equalities Office
GES	Gender Equality Scheme
GLA	Greater London Authority
GLC	Greater London Council
GPfA	Global Platform for Action
IDeA	Improvement and Development Agency
INGO	International Non-Governmental Organisation
LEA	Local Education Authority
LGB	Lesbian, Gay and Bisexual
LGBT	Lesbian, Gay, Bisexual and Transgender
MP	Member of Parliament
NAWO	National Alliance of Women's Organisations
NEETS	Not in Education, Employment or Training
NGO	Non-Governmental Organisation
OWN	Older Women's Network
PSED	Public Sector Equality Duty

SBS	Southall Black Sisters
TUC	Trades Union Congress
UN	United Nations
WLM	Women's Liberation Movement
WNC	Women's National Commission

1 Introduction

The way that public services are governed, resourced and delivered is crucial to women's lives. The provision of state funded care services, where they exist, represents perhaps one of the most transformative advances in gendered social relations and equality for women. But the cost of providing public services has, for decades, been a concern for governments around the globe, which is periodically intensified in times of economic crisis. The responsibility for either directly providing or commissioning publicly funded care services is most often devolved to the local state, making it a key site of feminist activity, but also the front line for public spending cuts more recently referred to as austerity measures. This book contributes to research on the history of social policy, legislation, strategy and practices for promoting gender equality within and through the local state. It is intended to be a timely contribution to debate on how transformational feminist political strategy can be sustained in the context of neo-liberal encroachment on welfare and public services in the name of austerity. In this chapter we introduce the lens through which we engaged with our research subject: the transformative potential for women's equality within the governance and provision of public services, of a particular piece of legislation, the Gender Equality Duty, in the context of continuity and change in gender equality work in local government.

The research

The research project which forms the basis of this book began in 2006 when the two authors shared the belief that something significant was about to happen in the struggle for gender equality in the UK. This was the enactment of a new piece of legislation, the Gender Equality Duty (GED), which we and many activists believed heralded a ground breaking step forward for women's equality. This optimism was shared by the Equal Opportunities Commission (EOC), the body that had been set up to champion gender equality in the first wave of equality legislation in the 1970s, who described the GED as the most important advance in women's equality in Great Britain since the Sex Discrimination Act 1975 (EOC, 2006). The legislation was ground breaking for a number of reasons, feminist and legal, that are discussed throughout the book.

The GED, like the other two equality duties for race and disability that preceded it, applied only to public authorities, which again felt significant to the authors as our research and our own feminist activism has focused on the welfare state and public services as a site of central importance for women's equality. Women's equality can be enabled by government funded services that support women's self-organisation and autonomy, free women from unpaid care in the family, provide substantial opportunities for paid work and provide safer environments for women to live in. Moreover, women's participation in local democracy and management are a means to challenge predominant constructs of gender, sexuality, race and class within welfare services, and to promote equality through redistribution of resources.

The GED was designed to promote equality in relation to both employment and service delivery, thus recognising the centrality of both for women's equality. These principles are generally accepted by feminists and policy makers in the twenty-first Century, but they were established only following the struggles of what has become known as second wave feminism. Much of the fight for improvements in women's lives during this period took place within and around public services. This context is important for understanding why the GED had the potential to be what Cockburn (1989) described as transformative. The GED and the other two duties for race and disability were combined in the Equality Act 2010 into a single Public Sector Equality Duty (PSED) that also encompassed other equality strands on religion and belief, age, sexuality gender reassignment, pregnancy and maternity. Although the expansion to these additional equality strands looked positive, the timing of the Equality Act coincided with the election of another strident neo-liberal government and the potential contained in the GED has been eroded successively since 2010. It is, therefore, equally important to understand why the loss of the GED and of what the public sector equality duties hoped to achieve represents, in our view, such a setback for equality, particularly women's equality.

Although the public sector equality duties are a particularly British phenomenon, we argue that the conceptual and political development they represented and their subsequent demise has repercussions for the way that the global struggle for equality is played out. Our analysis is particularly relevant at a time when equality legislation and policy are recognised to be failing, and the organisation of public services and local government are rapidly changing in the context of global economic crises. Women are the disproportionate casualties of reduced public service expenditure, which threatens to undo much of the work of promoting women's equality in and through public services and local government. The plight of women's equality in UK local government is all the more poignant because the introduction of the GED in 2007 seemed to herald the next positive phase in promoting equality for women as users and producers of public services. Instead the current economic outlook for public services and for women in developed and developing worlds looks bleaker than at any time since the post-war period.

The GED and other public sector equality duties share many of the characteristics of reflexive legislation (Fredman, 2001; McCrudden, 2007; Hepple, 2011).

The concept of reflexive legislation has its roots in theories of evolutionary law developed by US academics (Nonet and Selznick, 1978/2001) and reflexive law in Europe (Teubner, 1983). Nonet and Selznick propose an evolutionary spectrum, in which legislation moves through phases of development from restrictive to autonomous and eventually to responsive law. Restrictive law is coercive, designed to protect the individual pursuit of private interests and therefore benefits powerful elites. Autonomous law represents greater legal intervention required by the development of welfare states to regulate markets and provides a legitimising function which can be lost in restrictive law. Autonomous law simply separates substantive and procedural aspects of the law with the judiciary controlling the procedural whilst powerful polities still control the substantive. The autonomy of the law is still therefore partial. In contrast, the role of responsive law is to redistribute power by allowing for greater participation of those who will be affected by the law, making it more democratic (Selznick and Cotterrell, 2004); a quality we argue was intended to be a defining feature of the public sector equality duties.

Building on the work of Nonet and Selznick, Teubner (1983) develops the concept of reflexive law, arguing that such legislation requires a consideration of the interplay between the law and changing social structures. Teubner describes reflexive legislation as seeking to 'design self-regulating social systems through norms of organisation and procedure. Reflexive law, unlike formal law, does not accept "natural" subjective rights. Rather, it attempts to guide human action by redefining and redistributing property rights' (1983: 254–55). These theories have largely been gender neutral but they have some resonance with feminist arguments, that the state has both coercive and liberating potential, which we draw on throughout the book. Interestingly Nonet and Selznick argue that responsive legislation, because it redistributes power, is risky for state elites, which holds some further resonance with our analysis of the political reaction to the GED and its successor the Public Sector Equality Duty. Our research, therefore, provides a rare empirical study of these theoretical dynamics as they relate to women's equality work in the local state to implement the GED.

Research methodology

The research study that forms the core of this book, funded by the British Academy, set out to investigate how the GED was being implemented in five local authorities in England.[1] Each local authority was unique, in terms of geographical location and history, political administration, development of operational strategy for implementing equality policy, history of feminist organising, and at a different stage of implementation of the GED. We were interested in how equality practitioners had engaged with changing political and economic contexts to develop strategy and practices for promoting equality. More specifically we investigated the structures and drivers that had been used to implement the GED within local authorities, the key actors and formal and informal processes through which gender equality was negotiated, along with the interpretive/policy instruments and knowledge resources from which they drew. Our aim was to contribute to feminist research on how women's and gender equality could be advanced in, through and sometimes against the local state. Our research methods consisted largely of qualitative interviews with a range of actors (an elected member, senior executive officers, service delivery managers, trade unionists, equality officers, voluntary sector activists) who were engaged at a number of levels with the implementation of the GED in each of our case study authorities. We supplemented this data with documentary analyses of equality schemes and policies drawn up in relation to the GED. The book places our empirical research in its lived historical context and Chapter 4 draws on oral history interviews conducted by Margaret Page with equality activists working in the local state and beyond in the 1980s and 1990s.

Equalities advisors within the case study organisations viewed the research as a timely opportunity for more in-depth discussion of the likely impact of a single equalities approach and provided access to key personnel and documents to inform the research. However, since the research was completed, reorganisation and cuts in funding have led to the disbanding of two of the equality units, while the future of the third was uncertain. Regional equality networks in the fourth case study have lost their funding. This loss of resource in the form of knowledge and experience of practice and strategy for promoting equality and implementing legislation raises serious concerns and questions about the future.

Feminist activism is the focus of this book, but we recognise that feminism is not a unitary concept. The labels of radical, socialist and liberal feminism have been used, mostly by academics, to distinguish different feminist approaches. We utilise and explore these distinctions throughout the book. Interestingly, in the course of our research all of the women and some of the men we interviewed described themselves as feminists without feeling the need to locate this within a particular approach. We support arguments that the distinctions between different feminisms are often blurred when feminism is put into practice. None-the-less if we, as academics, were to label our feminism, it would fall closest to socialist feminism. In our view world-wide feminist struggle cannot be separated from the economic context of capitalism and political context of neo-liberalism. This is not to say that what happens between women and men within the private sphere is unimportant, but this too, we argue throughout the book, is influenced by the economic and political most often via differentiated intervention by the state.

Although as authors we share a similar feminist perspective, we bring experience and scholarship from different back grounds. Margaret Page brought to the research project her memories of doing equality work in local government in a variety of different roles during the period preceding the research study. She had been one of the first two women's equality advisors in a women's unit in a Left Labour London local authority in the 1980s, and had experienced the difficulty of negotiating contested visions for transformative change that informed equality work at that time. As co-author and researcher she wanted to find a way of writing that captured how equality practitioners had actively engaged with changing contexts in their strategies and practices, and the values, aspirations and passions that inspire and constrain equality work. Hazel Conley's experience is grounded in working-class politics and socialist-feminist activism in the trade union movement. As a researcher her interests have concerned the multiple roles of the state, but particularly as the major employer of women. Her more recent work has focused on equality legislation, particularly the GED and Public Sector Equality Duty, as both barrier and enabler for feminists and trade unionists.

Our methodological approach, inspired by feminist action inquiry (Reason and Bradbury, 2001; Maguire, 2001; Marshall, 1999) enabled us, within the research and through the co-authoring process, to adopt a critical and reflexive stance towards experiences of promoting women's equality that we brought to the research. As co-researchers we travelled to and from jointly held interviews and responded differently in the moment to what we saw. Conducting the field work together stimulated lively dialogue between us that informed our conversation with research participants, within interviews and informal discussions, as we each spoke from experiences in activist and professional roles that were located in different temporal and political contexts. This dialogue has continued into our co-authoring, as we discuss and analyse reports on the impact of austerity measures and of proposed welfare reform on women, the use of the equality legislation by activists and local strategies for resistance. A core strand of inquiry has been our conceptualisation of feminist struggle in relation to the local state. 'In and against the local state', a term first coined by the London Edinburgh Return Group in 1979, captures the outward facing stance which emerged from the first initiatives to mobilise state power to promote women's equality in the 1980s. Newman's (2012) concept of 'working the spaces of power' refers to how women who had entered politics and positions of power following the marketisation of public services, and accompanying changes in accountability and governance, were able to hold the tension between their vision of feminist equality and organisational accountabilities and values. What metaphor would adequately capture the project of mobilising state power to promote and protect gender equality in a context of neo-liberalism and concomitant movements for citizen and gender empowerment? This question goes to the heart of the dialogue we have maintained throughout our research and is taken up within each chapter of our co-authored text.

Our research and co-authoring partnership is grounded in a shared stance of feminist activism and the analysis we develop draws from feminist research in social policy, organisation studies, sociology and industrial relations. As co-authors we held two lenses in our approach to the research and the analysis of the data. The first was an inquiry into how the legislation, the GED, might take forward the struggle for gender equality in local government. Alongside this was an inquiry into how practitioners were interpreting the GED, within a changing political context. These two lenses were grounded in our distinctive experiences of holding in tension activism, our institutional loyalties and allegiances, and the methodological and disciplinary frameworks that we each brought to the research and co-authoring. In each of these our stance is one of aspiration for a transformative approach to gender equality work in local authorities, while asserting the need to hold open radical scepticism for its potential, in any specific context.

The book

The book begins with the theoretical context of our research on gendered social relations in welfare states generally and the local state specifically before moving on to the presentation of our empirical data in Chapters 4 and 5. Our concluding chapter considers our research findings and the prospects for transformative feminist activism in the context of economic austerity.

Chapter 2 introduces the key themes that are explored in greater detail throughout the rest of the book. It examines gendered social relations at the level of the welfare state as the conceptual site of public service provision. The chapter takes an international perspective and emphasises how political choices, rather than economic disasters, affect women's lives in particular ways. Feminist theory has traditionally distinguished between the coercive state that reinforces male breadwinner models of the family that disadvantage women and the liberating state where social policy and legislation are used to defamilise (Lister, 1994) structures that lock women into the 'private sphere'. Whilst we argue in the following chapters that the distinction between the coercive and liberating state is blurred because the coercive power of the state is necessary to realise its liberating potential, we also argue that in either its coercive or liberating mantle the state treats women differently to men and some women differently to others. This is a fundamental social relation that is obscured by equality discourses where women as a distinct social category are often absent. In addition we have emphasised feminist arguments that identify other dimensions to the politics of difference relating to ethnicity, religion, sexuality, marital status, age, disability, citizenship and place of birth, which determine how the state relates to women. We argue that whilst the tensions between the coercive and liberating state have provided a space for feminist activism to develop both locally and internationally from within and outside the state, the politics of difference has added a complexity to organising that has not been easy to translate into strategy and is an on-going challenge for feminist movements.

In Chapter 3 our theoretical focus moves to the local state to investigate how the research debates presented in Chapter 2, on the history of feminist engagement with welfare and public services, have been taken up in the specific context of feminist equality practice in local authorities in Great Britain. The chapter provides an historical account, drawn from feminist research, of how feminist activists in Great Britain have worked 'in and against the state' to develop public services that benefit women during the first decades of women's and gender equality work, beginning in the 1980s and ending with the introduction of the Public Sector Equality Duty in 2010. It demonstrates that in its first phases, the vision for women's equality within public services was firmly located within broad Leftist alliances to extend local democracy. The practices that were pioneered broke new ground in developing institutional structures and processes to promote the participation of women from a wide range of backgrounds in the governance, design and delivery of public services. We show that in the face of political adversity, feminist equality practitioners engaged strategically with a changing political landscape in which modernisation and marketisation were political ideologies used by both Conservative and Labour governments to restructure the organisation and ethos of public services. The chapter focuses on the architecture that equality practitioners developed to embed equality legislation within the political and management structures of local government and public services and analyses how modernisation of the local state led to shifts in the rationale for doing equality work from 'municipal feminism' to a justification predicated on a business case. The GED emerged from this seemingly inhospitable political context as a glimmer of hope for feminist activists and the chapter considers its short but promising history before charting its incorporation into a weakened form in the Equality Act 2010. The chapter offers a conceptual base and a context for the two chapters that follow, where we present research findings that investigate dilemmas and challenges experienced by equality practitioners as they reflect on their lived experiences of doing women's and gender equality work, attempting to harness the coercive power of the state for the benefit of women, prior to and during the implementation of the GED.

In Chapters 2 and 3 we discuss the potential and risks of harnessing state power to promote women's equality and how these highlight the inevitable tensions between feminist movement aspirations and state administrations nationally and locally. In Chapter 4 we begin our empirical investigation of the risks and opportunity that came with the contested nature of equality work, the collective vision, passion and resilience required to sustain it, and how this both supported and placed its own limitations on what was essentially a collaborative political project.

The chapter presents the findings of a co-inquiry with feminists who in a variety of roles were actively promoting gender equality in Left Labour local authorities during the moment of municipal feminism in the 1980s up to implementation of the GED in 2007. The participants reflect on the transformational feminist stance that inspired their gender equality work, the political tensions and conflicts they negotiated and the strategies and practices they developed. Their narratives bring to life the conceptual discussion of risk and opportunity of feminist engagement with the local state in Chapters 2 and 3. While based on memories that were partial and specific, they affirm the contribution that women's and gender equality work made to the development of an extended local democracy in which women in diverse local communities played an active part, and in which resources were directed towards services to meet women's specific self-defined priorities. This chapter shows that while women's equality work in these early decades prefigured in many ways the business case and 'customer focus' that was introduced as part of the modernisation of public services, it differed in its radical challenge to gender relations. Re-imagining gender equality, and engaging with the politics of difference, was at the core of the vision of the early women's equality work. We show in Chapter 5 how this vision developed in the transition from politically driven to business discourses of equality.

Chapter 5 presents our analysis of the empirical data that is at the core of our research project. In it we investigate the potential of state power, in the form of the GED, to promote transformational agendas for gender equality in the local state. In five case studies we analyse accounts from a range of local authority personnel and independent activists on the strategies and practices they have developed to implement the GED in the local state. We analyse the dilemmas they experienced and achievements they describe. A core theme is how practitioners worked the relationship between transformational vision, located within feminist organisation and socialist democracy, and predominant neo-liberal business practices and equality discourses.

The research findings confront us with a paradox: the GED has enabled equality practitioners to develop mechanisms for embedding legal compliance and reward systems for promoting gender equality within business practice in local authorities, but independent feminist and community based organisation of the previous period has faded. Within local authorities, the predominant equality discourse is liberal and generic and gender equality is often interpreted as equivalence of need between men and women. The focus of gender equality work is on internal systems for mainstreaming gender equality into corporate and service based management processes, supported and encouraged by national benchmarking systems. The stance of equality advisors was no longer adversarial 'in and against the state' but closer to their being 'tempered radicals' (Meyerson and Scully, 1995), with loyalty to both their organisation and to feminist goals of women's equality. In the five case studies participants speak of strategy and practices they had developed to work the interface between feminist equality and neo-liberal discourses of equality, to negotiate legal, political and institutional accountabilities. The case studies demonstrate the precariousness of feminist achievements in a period of changing political administrations, restructuring and cutbacks in resources for equality work. The chapter marks the end of a period where there was a fit between explicitly feminist agendas and socialist political institutions committed, however inadequately, to a transformative equality project within the local state. We return full circle to reliance on political networks to defend institutional mechanisms and forms of promoting equality that have been developed, in the context of radical change in the governance and resources available to the local state.

In our final chapter we return to 'the dream' of gender equality; the utopian imagination in feminist activism that drove the early phase of equality work within and against the local state. Drawing on the work of post-structuralist and socialist feminists, we consider these arguments in relation to the politics of difference. We continue the theme of intersectional coalition building and what this might mean in relation to moving beyond building single utopias in the local state. The chapter returns to the metaphor with which the book began, 'harnessing' the coercive power state for liberatory purposes to promote women's equality in the local state. We reflect on how we might describe feminist engagement with state power and institutions in the context of austerity, rising social divisions and inequalities. We consider the challenge to neo-liberalism from emerging social movements, new forms of feminist activism and how far reflexive legislation might be a force for transformational change.

Note

1 The Duties are different in Scotland, Wales and Northern Ireland (see Chapter 3).

2 Women's equality and the welfare state

Contradictory political landscapes

Introduction

The history of feminist struggle has been shaped by world events and crises; war and the changing state of the economy are pivotal in highlighting the nature of gender relations in most societies. Both women's and men's lives are irrevocably shaped by these events, but in different ways and, whilst such crises are often portrayed as unavoidable, it is the political choices made in response to them that have the deepest impact on gender relations and the position of women. In the most extreme and brutal cases sexual violence against women is used as a weapon of war. Whilst these acts are, following extensive international feminist lobbying, quite rightly treated by most of the global community as war crimes, the economic and social control of gender relations by the state is still considered a legitimate and often necessary response, particularly to crisis. Comparative feminist research has drawn attention to differences in these responses between nation states (e.g. O'Connor *et al.*, 1999; Orloff, 1996; Sainsbury, 1994; Walby, 2007; Lenz, 2007). Researchers have argued that historical events, including the ways in which social relations have developed, shape state policies and the class (Maurice and Sellier, 1979; Esping-Andersen, 1990; Coffey and Thornley, 2009) and gender (Heitlinger, 1979, 1993; Watson, 1990; Hantrais, 1994; Cousins, 1999) based resistance that these responses provoke.

The state takes on multiple forms and touches women's lives in all of its guises (Cockburn, 1977). However the concept of the welfare state, because of its centrality to public service provision and, therefore, its particular position between the state and the family, is often the focus of feminist analysis. Early theories of gender and the welfare state focused on the coercive nature of the state and its role in producing and maintaining structures of oppression, largely capitalism and patriarchy, usually, ironically, as a provider of welfare (e.g. Wilson, 1977; Pateman, 1988). Later theories critiqued the essentialist nature of these arguments and stressed that state actions are political choices evident in differences in approach both within and between nation states (see Watson, 1990). This is not to say that capitalism and patriarchy are redundant concepts in understanding women's oppression. Capitalism, at least, is still at the core of social relations in arguably all advanced societies and economies, including most of those that still declare themselves to be socialist. Patriarchy, after more than a century of feminist activism, may manifest in less explicit ways in advanced capitalist economies but is still a daily reality for many millions of women.

The important point here, one that we explore in greater detail in the following chapters, is that political choices respond sometimes directly and sometimes indirectly to the needs of capital but always in gendered ways. Global capital has influenced the role of the nation state and, therefore, the welfare state in ways that particularly affect women (Hobson *et al.*, 2002; Walby, 2002; Franzway and Fonow, 2011). But government policy on welfare and equality also shapes and is shaped by the type and level of resistance the state encounters and by pressure for change from activists and ultimately, in democracies, by the electorate (Cooper, 1993). In later feminist theories of the welfare state, therefore, the role of the state is not static and fixed but dynamic and mutable (Eisenstein, 1981; Watson, 1990). Implicit in this view is that change is possible and that activism is the key. The type of change that might be hoped for remains a subject of debate as boundaries between reformist and transformative agendas and outcomes are often blurred in practice (Jewson and Mason, 1986) as are the distinctions between types of feminist activism (Cockburn, 1991; Lovenduski and Randall, 1993).

Most of the academic writing on gender and welfare states is based on developed economies. Authors who have written about welfare in developing economies usually highlight a more central role of the family and patriarchal relations and weaker state responses to welfare (e.g. Wong, 1998; Rai, 1999 cited in Lister, 2003).

This chapter and the one that follows provide the theoretical and political context for empirical data drawn from the UK that we present in Chapters 4 and 5. Our analysis concentrates on Western literature and begins by looking at theories of the role of the welfare state in restricting or promoting women's equality before moving on to an examination of the way in which activism shapes policies and processes to initiate positive change for women. The chapter also examines how gender research on welfare states has been critiqued and developed by ethnic minority, lesbian and disabled feminist writers and activists. The final section considers research on feminist activism and the welfare state as an important theoretical and empirical backdrop to our own research.

Defining the welfare state

Feminist literature on welfare states in the 1990s provided a critique of academic models that have failed to capture their gendered nature. Much of this critique was sparked by Esping-Andersen's *The Three Worlds of Welfare Capitalism*. In this influential book, Esping-Andersen (1990) highlights how political choices make it difficult to give one definition that fits all variants of welfare states. He instead provides a typology of three[1] ideal types of welfare regimes that have developed in what he describes as welfare capitalism. Although, for

Esping-Andersen, gender relations in welfare states are subsumed in the 'family', he does identify some common defining criteria:

> Notwithstanding the lack of purity, if our essential criteria for defining welfare states have to do with the quality of social rights, social stratification, and the relationship between state, market and family, the world is obviously composed of distinct regime-clusters.
>
> (Esping-Andersen, 1990, p.29)

The first of these clusters, the liberal regime, is meant to interfere as little as possible in capitalist markets, particularly labour markets. In this model the state provides the barest safety net between survival and destitution without offering an attractive alternative to paid employment. State provided benefits under this regime are limited both in terms of entitlement and value. Receipt of benefits is also often stigmatised as a drain on national resources. For Esping-Andersen, this model is seemingly gender neutral because the liberal view is that markets, if they are operating at optimum, are considered not to discriminate.

The second regime, which Esping-Andersen calls the corporatist welfare state, is conservative and upholds traditional values. Markets are secondary to the influence of the Church, hierarchy, status and the family. Esping-Andersen (p.27) notes that the centrality of these institutions has implications for women as care is expected to be provided in the home rather than by state-funded public services, except where there is irretrievable family break-down.

The third regime, the social-democratic model, has the most developed welfare systems provided by the state. Referring largely to the Scandinavian countries, the social-democratic model conceptualises the state as playing a major role in tempering the unpredictability of markets. The provision of welfare is not limited to a basic subsistence level and is universal, intended for both middle-class and working-class citizens. As such it is considered a social right rather than a drain on national resources. Extensive publicly funded services provide care as the norm rather than an emergency, which has a positive impact on women's labour market participation, discussed further below.

A key component of Esping-Andersen's theory of welfare state regimes is that the eventual form a regime takes is shaped by class resistance and the pressure it can bring to bear on governments. Interestingly he argues that no one single class can effectively force change but coalitions, usually between middle and working classes, can influence governments. Perhaps even more relevant for our purposes is Esping-Andersen's claim that the type and strength of class coalitions determine government actions in response to retrenchment and decline of welfare state policies (p.32).

The feminist critique

Feminist writers on the welfare state have criticised Esping-Andersen's model for failing to address gendered power and, in this sense, being 'gender blind'

(Orloff, 1993; O'Connor *et al.*, 1999; Lewis, 1997; Sainsbury, 1994; 1999; Walby, 2007; Osawa, 2007). Whilst our analysis above highlights that this is not entirely the case, only a cursory glance is directed to the differential impact welfare regimes might have on women. Furthermore, the failure to address gender is particularly the case in relation to liberal welfare regimes, of which Britain is considered to be an example. The first indication that the model is based largely on men's lives and experiences is its focus on labour market participation and paid work-related benefits, such as pensions. It is also the case that some of the key elements of the theory such as class coalition and decommodification do not differentiate between men and women, or allow for specifically gendered forms of resistance. The idea that the main role of the welfare state is to decommodify workers is particularly erroneous in relation to women. In Esping-Andersen's theoretical framework, welfare regimes provide undifferentiated workers with an alternative to complete reliance on selling their labour to capital for survival. In most economies women who are employed in full-time paid work for the whole of their adult lives are very much in the minority. The majority of women are therefore already decommodified, regardless of the existence of a welfare state, but rely on men's commodification for their survival. Indeed, in Esping-Andersen's framework, in the example of the most developed welfare regime, the social democratic model, the state seeks actively to commodify women's labour to reduce their reliance on men's earnings.

The basis of Esping-Andersen's analysis is that welfare regimes are differentiated but Orloff (1993) argues that the comparative analysis from which Esping-Andersen bases his three models does not reflect the differences between states that fall within the same regime in relation to their treatment of women. For example, the provision of state-funded childcare varies between Sweden and Norway with considerably reduced labour market access for Norwegian women, although they both fall within Esping-Andersen's social-democratic welfare regime. Similarly, Orloff claims the model cannot explain unexpected differences between regimes in relation to the outcomes for women, giving the example that, in 1993, women in Sweden, even with the most extensive provision of state provided care services, still did 72 per cent of unpaid household labour compared to 74 per cent of women in the US with the least state provided care services (ibid., p.313). Orloff contends that these analytical shortcomings stem from the error of concentrating only on power relations between the state, the market and the family whilst ignoring the power relations within the family.

In an earlier analysis Eisenstein (1981) explores the inevitable tension between liberal and feminist strategies for gender equality, where liberalism constructs gendered domestic relations as 'natural' and 'private' in contrast to the feminist project of transforming gender relations within domestic, social and economic spheres. The lack of engagement with gender relations in relation to liberal regimes in Esping-Andersen's model similarly results from a failure to consider the tensions between liberal political philosophy and feminist theory. One of the central tenets of liberal thought is the separation of the public and private domains of social life, with the strong belief that the state should interfere as little as possible in the private lives of its citizens. This separation and abstentionism has had a profound impact on the lives of women for a number of reasons. Separation does not disturb the traditional, conservative conceptualisation of the family headed by a man but serviced by a woman, whilst abstentionism removes the likelihood of change. Therefore, whilst the liberal logic of separating the state from the family is one of protecting the freedom of genderless citizens from an overbearing state, for women the separation simply locks in unequal power relations in the family.

Despite this analysis, change has occurred and women's lives have improved, so how might this be explained? Firstly, O'Connor *et al.* (1999) argue that liberalism has taken different forms at various historical junctures and in different states. They distinguish between classical liberalism, new liberalism, social policy liberalism and contemporary neo-liberalism. Classical liberalism equates roughly to a period that stretches from the enlightenment to, in the UK, the early twentieth century. During this time the principles of liberal philosophy were developed and established in social, political and economic policy. O'Connor *et al.* note that whilst classical liberalism was a reaction to traditionalism and conservatism, new liberalism was a response to the continuing class and gender inequalities reinforced by classical liberalism and market relations. Pressure for change came from the development of a strong labour movement and an active and organised women's movement in the early twentieth century. Notably, new liberalism allowed a greater role for the state in creating a more equal society, essentially paving the way in the UK for the modern welfare state and Keynesian economic policy. O'Connor *et al.* note that, whilst this turn in liberal policy meant change was possible and some important gains for women were made, the breadwinner model of the family was left largely intact (O'Connor *et al.*, 1999).

Feminist critics have argued that if gender relations as well as class relations are considered when theorising the welfare state, then the dynamic, fluid and context specific relationship between the state, capital and patriarchy must be considered. The state constructs and shapes gender relations through social policy, fiscal and welfare regimes. The breadwinner model, for example, is based on women's unpaid work within the home and a single primary breadwinner paid a 'family wage' within a heterosexual family. Alternatively, state-provided care services, jobs and equality legislation have the potential to free women from economic dependence on a male partner, even if liberation stretches only as far as being reliant on capital for wages to the same extent as men. The following sections explore the coercive and liberating potential of welfare states from feminist perspectives.

The coercive state

Despite historical differences between nation states, there are some enduring similarities in gendered social relations. The location of women in the home assigned the responsibility for care of men, children and elders is common in all societies, although to varying degrees, usually depending on how far the state intervenes. Second wave feminist writers from around the globe have documented how, in times of crisis, women are encouraged into the public sphere and then pushed out of it or, in industrialised and industrialising societies, retained as a cheap and 'flexible' segment of the labour market as part of the political and economic response. The role of the state in supporting a male breadwinner model of the family has been pivotal in all cases, even if managed by different states in different ways. Feminist writing in the 1970s and 80s was concerned with challenging moral arguments about the needs of the family, the home and the sanctity of marriage, identifying how these anchors of patriarchy have been used instrumentally by the state. For some feminists, the control of women's bodies, largely in relation to reproductive rights and sexuality, was the focus of concern (e.g. MacKinnon, 1989). The focus for others was how these institutions were a means to justify interventions to control women's paid labour and their unpaid labour in the reproduction of labour power.

Pateman (1988) illustrates the relationship between patriarchy and capital by drawing comparisons between the marriage contract and the employment contract. It is argued that what appear to be mutually advantageous arrangements for both parties are in fact relationships based on social inequality; both involve an exchange of property in the form of obedience based on the unequal power balance between the parties. In women's employment the two combine to produce a particularly effective form of subordination. A graphic illustration of this point is the marriage bar, which was a formal feature of civil service employment until 1946, but continued informally for much longer (Cockburn, 1991). Glucksmann argues that a formal marriage bar was a particular feature of certain forms of public sector employment:

> The legally enforced marriage bar covered all local government and civil service employment, including teaching and most other office work. In professional and non-manual occupations work was not so physically arduous as in a factory, and women were likely to be better-off financially and in a better position to afford labour saving domestic appliances ... In their situation then, waged or salaried employment was more compatible with domestic responsibility. Hence the need for a formal marriage bar: if married women were to be removed, forcible means were necessary to achieve the end.
> (Glucksmann, 1990, p.223)

Clearly the state as employer has a history of placing limits on women's employment contracts that would have been considered unthinkable for men. But the state, it has been argued, uses its institutional powers extensively to maintain patriarchal structures that cast women as dependents in the service of the family and of the state, and in this sense the development of the welfare state substitutes private patriarchy for public patriarchy (Walby, 1990). Wilson (1977) argued that the development of the modern welfare state in the UK was based on assumptions that women are the shock absorbers of crisis – individually in the home and collectively in the nation. This position was assured in the past by making women financially dependent on men throughout their adult lives by limiting access to employment directly via marriage bars and indirectly by limited provision of child and elder care; supporting the concept of a family wage paid directly to men and limiting women's contributions to national insurance schemes and, therefore, access to most welfare benefits and the state pension.

Feminist economists have challenged the separation between domestic and social and economic spheres by asserting the economic contribution made by domestic labour in the home (e.g. Waring, 1988, 1995). In 1993, the UN revised the system of national accounts to recommend that all production of goods in households for their own consumption be included in the measurement of economic output, a definition excluding childcare, elder-care, cooking and cleaning. Some countries have adopted measures to include caring responsibilities in GDP, thereby providing an economic rationale for welfare that supports and enables women's independence.[2] Cousins (1999) points out that, by the end of the twentieth century, the worst gendered inequalities in state benefits had been removed during periods of welfare reform usually prompted by feminist activity, but change has been faltering and contradictory with tensions visible from the outset. For example, in the UK, whilst the 1942 Beveridge plan, which underpinned the development of the post-war welfare state, was infused with a breadwinner model of the family (Lister, 2003), the marriage bar for women teachers was removed in 1944. Similarly legislative reform on contraception, abortion and divorce came relatively early in the UK in the mid-1960s and early 1970s but the equality legislation of the 1970s, which led eventually to the removal of the most blatant forms of sex discrimination from welfare payments, required external political pressure to meet European legislative requirements (Cousins, 1999; Walby, 2007). These early gains were followed by economic crises in the 1980s and 90s which led to attacks on public spending and changes to social policy that began to return responsibility for the care of elderly and vulnerable dependents back to the family, meaning most often the unpaid labour of women (Coote and Campbell, 1982; Lovenduski and Randall, 1993; Cousins, 1999). Similar patterns can be observed in more recent times; whilst, as we argue in the following chapters, legislative reform on gender equality in the UK looked positive in 2007, cuts to public sector spending on welfare in response to global economic crisis meant that by 2012 the general secretary of the TUC declared that the coalition government was 'the most women unfriendly in living memory'.[3]

Just as differences in gender regimes between welfare states suggest that welfare can offer opportunities for women's equality, so too the continuities point to underlying patterns of gender inequality to be addressed through feminist struggle within both democratic and non-democratic states and capitalist and non-capitalist economies. For example, Cousins (1999) notes the centrality of the breadwinner model throughout Europe, including Franco's Spain and East Germany prior to unification. In all cases this model had started to weaken towards the end of the twentieth century, albeit with wide variations. Similar patterns are evident in Australia (Sainsbury, 1994; Eisenstein, 1996; O'Connor *et al.* 1999; Cousins, 1999) and North America (Sainsbury, 1994; Orloff, 1993; O'Connor *et al.* 1999).

The liberating state

Although Wilson's (1977) classic book on women and the welfare state in the UK focuses on the coercive nature of the state, there is an acceptance in the closing pages that the welfare state might also have some positive effect on the lives of women. A similar message can be taken from Pateman's (1988) work. The contradictory nature of gender relations within the state continued to be analysed by the London Edinburgh Weekend Return Group[4] (1979), who argued that most citizens, but particularly women, rely at some stage of their lives on the state for economic independence from what would otherwise be total vulnerability under capitalist social relations. In their work the group raised the additional tension of state workers who are charged with implementing the kind of public service delivery that might not be in their interests as a class and as women, ethnic minorities, as people with disabilities or with different sexualities:

> the social worker, or nurse or teacher is in a similar situation at work to that in which she is (and others are) as mother or lover at home. She loves and cares because she is human. But that loving and caring is doubly exploited. It seems to involve her in unpaid and unfair amounts of work in the home. And it causes her to accept underpaid and often heartbreaking work outside. Yet if she resists, she risks hurting herself and the people she cares about, merely to ruffle the state a little.
>
> (London Edinburgh Weekend Return Group, 1979, p.44)

The inevitability of contestation and compromise between what women hope for from public services and the reality of what can be negotiated in any given context is an issue which has central importance for our research and the arguments in this book, and one we will return to often and from different perspectives in the following chapters.

Although the London Edinburgh Weekend Return Group highlights the contradictory nature of the welfare state, their overall prognosis is negative: that the state mobilises its coercive powers to protect established gender relations and women's unpaid labour role in the family. As we have already argued, context needs to be taken into consideration and the group was writing at a time when neo-liberal political reform of public services in the UK was already well underway and hurtling towards Thatcherism. In contrast research outside the UK, largely in the Scandinavian countries, argued that the contradiction evident in welfare states could be harnessed to favour a more progressive approach for women. Hernes (1987, 1988) argued that Nordic welfare states have demonstrated more 'woman-friendly' and 'state feminist' tendencies. In Denmark Siim (1988) argued that women were cast as consumers of public services rather than dependent on public services. This has been achieved by the transfer of aspects of care, largely in relation to the young, the old and the sick, away from the family and into publicly funded services, a process later to be described by Lister (1994) as 'defamilization'. The liberating state, it is argued, simultaneously freed women from unpaid work in the home and provided women with paid work delivering the public services that are created. There is some parallel in the UK in the 1970s where expansion of state services created jobs for women and care services (Coote and Campbell, 1982) (see Chapter 3).

It is important to note that Hernes placed feminist activism, both at 'grass-roots' and at elite levels, as central to achieving positive change. But even in Scandinavian countries the ambivalent relationship between the state, the family and capital is evident. Providing a useful historical analysis, Cousins (1999) notes that in Sweden, although reforms to welfare provision were prompted by low birth rates in the 1930s, at that time policy was largely designed to support women inside the home by making transfer payments to discourage the need for women to provide a second income from work outside the home. Women's participation in paid work was not directly supported and did not increase significantly until the economic boom of the 1960s when there was increased demand for women's labour in Sweden's burgeoning private sector industry. In response the focus of social policy shifted to state provided and subsidised childcare outside the home, allowing and encouraging women to take up paid employment. In taking this approach, the Scandinavian model moved away from a breadwinner model, with clear delineations between the earning and caring roles of men and women, to a dual earner and carer model in which gendered roles become more fluid. It should be emphasised, however, that there is a good deal of variation between Scandinavian states.

Esping-Andersen's (2009) later work which, in answer to feminist critique of his earlier theories, does focus on women, offers an interesting and controversial twist to the concept of the liberating welfare state. In this work, Esping-Andersen argues that women's liberation from the home has only benefitted middle-class women and the 'incomplete revolution' is damaging to society because working-class families, particularly children, are suffering greater inequality as a result. The welfare state, as in Scandinavian models and particularly the Danish case, is, in Esping-Andersen's view, necessary to bridge the inequality gap between middle-class and working-class women. Therefore, although women are central to this work, it is still class and not gendered social relations between men and women, outside or within the family, that result in women's inequality. Inter-estingly, in this addition to Esping-Andersen's earlier theories, *men* are largely absented because it is considered that they are unlikely to share enough of the domestic labour to allow working-class women to join the revolution. Indeed if they did so, Esping-Andersen argues, the case for a liberating welfare state would be diminished (ibid., p.90). Therefore, perhaps it is worth extrapolating that the liberating potential of the welfare state rather unexpectedly benefits men as they get to enjoy the financial gains of having a working partner without having to share the burden of domestic responsibilities. Not surprisingly Esping-Andersen's (2009) focus on women in welfare capitalism has drawn further feminist critique.

Returning to the work of feminist authors, attention has been drawn to the limitations of Scandinavian models (Borchorst and Siim, 2002; Melby *et al.*, 2009). One criticism is that the model concentrates women's labour in paid caring work in the state sector and that care in the home remains primarily the responsibility of women. So much so that Jenson (1997, p.183) argues: 'In Sweden, then, the male breadwinner model is weak, but the female caregiver model is hegemonic.' Gendered divisions of labour therefore remain intact and underpin segregated and segmented labour markets, which in turn fuel pay and other labour market inequalities (Hirdman, 1990 cited in Borchorst and Siim, 2008). Further critiques have highlighted that, as neo-liberal political ideology has started to permeate these states, so too has the 'woman-friendliness' of social policy come under pressure. The restructuring of public services that epitomises neo-liberal policy has touched the Scandinavian states in the form of marketisation and 'new public management' (Cousins, 1999; Borchorst and Siim, 2008).

Gender segregation in public service employment means that women are particularly vulnerable to neo-liberal retrenchment and restructuring of the welfare state. Researchers have pointed out that where welfare provision has been minimal and childcare is provided by the market, as in the USA, women have not been subjected to these particular vulnerabilities in employment. Furthermore, some research studies found that US affirmative action programmes started to make some progress in reducing occupational segregation (Sainsbury, 1994; Orloff, 1993; O'Connor *et al.*, 1999), although Esping-Andersen (1990, p.226) warns that the extent of these programmes needs to be treated with caution. A further criticism is that affirmative action programmes only benefit working women, whilst women who do not work and are public service users are the target of increasingly stringent welfare-to-work programmes that reinforce occupational gender and racial segregation (Hancock, 2004). In the UK case, many women rely on public sector employment, have limited access to subsidised childcare but have none of the benefits of affirmative action. They are increasingly subject to welfare-to-work policies and are facing a particularly damaging combination of vulnerabilities as the welfare state is starved of resources as a response to financial crisis (Women's Budget Group, 2013; Fawcett Society, 2012).

It is clear that, although the concept of the welfare state is built on similar assumptions about the family and care and is underpinned by the same tensions in relation to capitalism in different nation states, these are mediated by governments in different ways. Comparative feminist researchers have highlighted how political choices result in different outcomes for women. In more recent research, they are sensitive to the criticism that the category 'woman' is not unitary. So, whilst there are differences between states in their approach to welfare and public services, there are also differences within states in relation to social divisions beyond class and gender regarding who should benefit from the welfare state and who should deliver it, which are explored in more detail below.

Welfare states and the politics of difference

The breadwinner model is predicated on a conceptualisation of the family as consisting of an able-bodied, heterosexual couple and their children where the father is the main wage earner and the mother works unpaid in the home, a concept Abramovitz (1996, p.3) termed the 'family ethic'. The rise of the dual career family has introduced more flexibility in gender roles in the family, but has not changed the overall division of labour in the home. At the heart of the model are issues of class, ethnicity, gender and sexuality, but there are other intersections relating to religion, marital status, age, disability, citizenship and place of birth. These intersections remain visible even when the basic model has been reconfigured through welfare provision and social policy, for example, in the Scandinavian states.

O'Connor *et al.* (1999) show how the structural principle of most welfare states to draw a separation between social insurance based welfare and dependency based welfare, leads to different treatment between women and men *and* between different groups of women. Social insurance based welfare is based on contributions made from earnings meant to provide a decent standard of living following retirement or short periods of involuntary unemployment. Dependency based welfare is often provided as the minimal 'safety net' between survival and destitution. This separation is a remnant of Victorian notions of the deserving and the undeserving poor and O'Connor *et al.* (ibid.) argue that, whilst social insurance based welfare is conceptualised and treated as a right and the 'norm', dependency based welfare is given grudgingly and conceptualised as a drain on national resources (see also Fraser and Gordon, 1994). Those who have complied with the breadwinner model are rewarded, men through their employment and therefore insurance contribution record and women by their employment record and/or marriage to men with such a record. Women who live outside the breadwinner model, for example, single mothers, have gained particular opprobrium when relying on the state for support (Gordon, 1994).

An important strand of this literature has argued that these separations are not only gendered but they are also ethnicised. Building on the black feminist critique of feminist theory a number of authors have highlighted how welfare regimes are an important spoke in the wheel of racial stereotypes (e.g. Hill-Collins, 1998; Hancock, 2004; Gordon, 1994). Hill-Collins (1998, p.65) argues that the family, core of the breadwinner model, is the primary site of gendered and racial hierarchy:

> Whereas White men and White women enjoy shared racial privileges provided by Whiteness, within the racial boundary of Whiteness, women are expected to defer to men. People of color have not been immune from this same logic. Within the frame of race as family, women of subordinated racial groups defer to men of their groups, often to support men's struggles in dealing with racism.

Hill-Collins goes on to illustrate how these hierarchies have been replicated in the US welfare system with the divide between social insurance and welfare dependency acting as a site of racial segregation. These divisions were historically created, it is argued, by government policies that expected black women, unlike white women, to work throughout their lives but which used occupational segregation to exclude their work from social insurance provisions forcing them, when they could not work, into welfare dependency.

The experience of ethnic minority women has varied depending on the history and circumstances of their exploitation. Hill-Collins' work holds for African-American women who are still oppressed by the historical legacy of slavery, whilst the experience of Native American women reflects their different struggle against segregation, involuntary sterilisation, the forced removal of children, addiction and criminalisation (Lawrence, 2000; Ross, 2005). The different treatment of aboriginal women in Canadian and Australian welfare systems (Flick, 1990; Wanganeen, 1990) has also been noted. In the UK and the Scandinavian nations the racialisation of welfare is strongly linked to immigration. Abramovitz (1996), for example, argues that immigrant women are forced to work because of extreme poverty caused by exclusion from entitlement to welfare benefits, and through immigration policy that restricts familial migration and the rights of female partners to citizenship. In many cases immigrant women provide the domestic labour for dual career families, providing a bridge between public and private spheres for women wealthy enough to employ them.

The model of the breadwinner family utilised by most states is inherently heterosexual. As Lind (2004) argues, 'policy struggles over the meaning of family and attacks on LGBT communities and civil rights have gone hand-in-hand' (p.22). Lesbians, and in particular lesbian mothers, are treated very differently from heterosexual women in welfare states, which became a key focus for feminist campaigns and contestation in relation to state and welfare provision in the UK (Chapter 3). Key issues include access to reproductive health and care services for lesbians (Hartman, 2005), custody of children of lesbian mothers (Arnup 1989; Shapiro, 1996), fostering and adoption for lesbian couples (e.g. Hick, 2000, 2005; Brooks and Goldberg, 2001; Gates *et al.*, 2007), immigration and legal status for lesbian and gay couples and the faltering steps to legislate for same sex marriage (Lind, 2004). Cooper (1993, 1994) notes that whilst lesbian and gay campaigns have gained reform in some areas by tapping into liberal arguments around freedom and choice, radical lesbian feminists have fared less well where their demands and campaigns for sexual equality and reproductive rights have been too far removed from the hegemony of the heterosexual family (see also Colgan and Wright, 2011). In Chapters 3 and 4 we explore further how conflict between liberal and radical approaches to gender equality manifests within equality initiatives within Left Labour local authorities in Great Britain.

Although given much less attention in the academic feminist literature (Morris, 1992), women with disabilities are also treated differently by the state than women without disabilities (Mudrick, 1984; Russo and Jansen, 1984; Deegan and Brooks, 1985; Barnes and Mercer, 2005; Turner *et al.*, 2006), often because they do not fit easily within a breadwinner model as unpaid carers, or because of particularly restricted employment opportunities. Mudrick (1984) notes that in the USA, the distinction between insurance based benefits and welfare based benefits is most clearly evident in disability related payments. Russo and Jansen (1984) found that in the USA, women with disabilities were much less likely to be covered by pension and health insurance than disabled men. Furthermore, because a larger proportion of disabled women than non-disabled women are single heads of their household, they were less likely to be covered by a spouse's social insurance benefits. Disabled women were far more likely to be in receipt of welfare based support, but Mudrick argues that 'disabled women receive less from these public income support programs than disabled men, despite their often greater economic need' (Mudrick, 1984, p.245). Mudrick also makes the point that disability in the USA is further gender segregated by the higher status and payments awarded to military or war veterans.

Exclusion from the labour market and the restricted access to welfare payments means that disabled women are often amongst the poorest members of society and rely heavily on publicly funded services. Despite this, writing about the British welfare state, Morris (1998) makes the important point that the way public services are provided is often infused with gendered and able-ist assumptions about, for example, the ability of disabled women to care for their children, the provision of suitable housing, the education of disabled children and the accessibility of public transport. Morris (1993) argues that by focusing on women as carers, feminists have isolated women who are cared for and have consigned disabled women to institutionalised care to support the liberty of non-disabled women to seek paid work often, ironically, in the same publicly funded institutions. This argument could be extended to age-related disability and the care needs of older women who have spent their lives, and often their health, caring for others. Despite these criticisms Morris (1993) argues that, if positive change is to happen, alliances between disabled and non-disabled feminists must be made and that disability should be mainstreamed into feminist research.

The need for alliances for social change is a theme that has echoed through feminist activism and in both 'malestream' and feminist research on the state and the welfare state (see, for example, Albrecht and Brewer, 1990; Rowbotham *et al.*, 1979/2013). Esping-Andersen (1990) argues that alliances between classes have brought about change. The London Edinburgh Weekend Return Group called for alliances within the working class, between public service providers and users. Feminists have sought class alliances and hoped for alliances between women with different experiences of the welfare state to pursue change. Walby claims that 'there has been a move away from identity politics towards alliances, coalitions and networks' (Walby, 2011, p.78) that signals a change in feminist activism and praxis. But realising the need for alliance does not dissolve the tensions that underpin differences of power and does not guarantee success. Feminist demands for social and economic policies have grappled with disagreements about what they wanted the state to do, to take into account that the state relates differently to women according to their demographic and political situation, and to consider the way the state relates to women in different historical contexts. Within these debates social policy as much as law has been a site of political struggle (Rowbotham, 1990). Racist, heterosexist, able-ist and class-based practice in relation to immigration law, policing, fostering and adoption and the regulation of childcare, housing, reproductive health, mental health and education have all been sites of contestation and struggle (Curno *et al.*, 1982; see, for example, Mama, 1984, cited in Rowbotham, 1990, p.146; Parmar, 1982, cited in Rowbotham, 1990, p.159). Understanding how and when feminists have sought alliances to pursue women's equality in the welfare state and how, when and why they have sometimes succeeded and sometimes failed is considered in the remainder of this chapter and in the following chapter.

Feminist activism(s) and the welfare state

Despite the agreement that alliances are central to activism, feminism, particularly in the UK, is often defined by its conceptual divisions, usually categorised according to liberal, radical or socialist political philosophies that underpin various approaches to achieving women's equality (Cockburn, 1989, 1991; Lovenduski and Randall, 1993). Although it is now just as common to note the artificial nature of these distinctions in feminist praxis, there is still a propensity to fall back on them when critiquing forms of activism. Much of the debate between feminists has focused on how far activism should take place within the state and how far it should remain outside a male dominated and controlled polity (e.g. Eisenstein, 1996; Fraser, 2009; Walby, 2011). The radical feminist position has been to agitate outside the state and in direct opposition to it, but the majority of feminist activism has been either from within the state or lobbying for incremental change from the edges. Lovenduski and Randall (1993, p.7) sum this point up well:

> If few women claim to be Liberal feminists, many pursue Liberal feminist goals of seeking to promote and integrate women into public life in the hope that the implementation of feminist policies will follow. In the British context, Liberal feminism is perhaps better understood as a strategy rather than as a movement.

The term 'femocrat' was used by Australian feminist academics to describe the role of feminist activists who reached positions senior enough to influence change in government structures and policies. The term has both positive and pejorative uses with critics, both inside and outside the women's movement, using the term to indicate an elitist and self-interested activity, whilst the women in these positions have reclaimed the term to assert a position of feminist power (Chappell, 2002; Sawer, 1996; Eisenstein, 1996). Interestingly for our research, and something we return to in Chapter 3, writers on Australian femocracy of the 1970s and 80s highlight that one of their main operational strategies was to mainstream women's issues into government policies, operationalised by impact assessments at a time before mainstreaming was a feminist buzzword and well before very similar principles would be used to develop the Gender Equality Duty in Britain in the 2000s (see Sawer, 1996, p.6).

Writers on femocracy stress that it is a strategy option only available when there is enough political support to allow feminist women to get a foot in the political door. The consensus also seems to be that the nearer the government is to liberal or neo-liberal philosophy, the smaller the opportunity gap will be (see also Walby, 2011). In the UK and Australia this has meant that a femocratic strategy usually only operates successfully when there is a Labour government in power, with the proviso that Labour governments in recent history have moved closer to neo-liberal social and economic policies. Eisenstein (1996, p.13) argues that, because global economic conditions impact on women's labour market position and on government social policies that affect women, they also impact on feminist activism. These are issues that are relevant to our research and are considered in relation to the UK context in great detail in the following chapter.

There is a good deal of critical assessment of the Australian femocracy, as Eisenstein (1996, p.xv) notes, from both the right and the left of the political spectrum and from both inside and outside the feminist movement. The experiences of Julia Gillard as Australia's first woman Prime Minister are a vivid reminder of just how entrenched and damaging sexism is in the political sphere. Arguments from the right quite predictably accused the femocrats of attacking traditional family structures and for introducing bias in financial decision-making that sullied the role of the civil servant as objective and politically neutral (see Sawer, 1996, p.5) and introduced market imperfections. Conversely many feminists criticised femocrats for betraying the women's movement by adopting masculine ideals of hierarchy and elitism. This critique was extended by arguing that, rather than working towards transformative feminist objectives, femocrats were incorporated into what remained essentially male dominated and patriarchal state structures, leading to the alternative label of state feminism. It was further noted that the femocracy, like the malestream, was essentially white and middle-class and therefore could not and did not represent all women, raising again the issue of how to engage with the politics of difference. There are, of course, strong counter-arguments that are beyond the scope of the discussion here, but are considered further in relation to the UK context in the next chapter.

One of the advantages of developing defined processes and structures to support feminist activity within the state is the ability to extend these beyond the nation state to build international networks. When conditions at home are bleak for feminism, transnational protocols and funding programmes can provide leverage for developing local and national machinery for implementing gender equality. Some of these developments are considered below.

Transnational feminist activism and the arrival of gender mainstreaming

Feminist activists have consistently been shapers of transnational protocols, as well as using them to develop local, national and international machinery, whether as elected politicians, independent activists within social movements, civil servants or independent expert consultants (Newman, 2012; Walby, 2007, 2011; Lenz, 2007). The UN, the Council of Europe and the EU in particular have been the channels through which feminist activism, particularly under the aegis of gender mainstreaming, has been introduced into UK government policy. Furthermore, strategy and practice for gender mainstreaming has been developed within transnational partnerships funded by EU programmes. Many of these partnerships have brought together women's organisations with local authorities and trade unions.

The UN Decade of Women conferences that began in 1975 provided a focus for women's mobilisation at parallel, regional preparatory conferences and established the principle of negotiation between women's independent organisations and government on position statements. Feminist mobilisation gained momentum in 1995, when 30,000 women from five worldwide regions took part in the NGO Forum that paralleled the UN Fourth World Conference on Women in Beijing (Friedlander, 1996). Through these events a transnational gender equality policy network developed that was able to shape UN policy directives and continues to provide leverage for calling national governments to account, both on policy issues and on developing governmental equality machinery (Squires, 2007; Walby, 2011).

The processes developed for participation were often powerfully rooted in women's life experiences at local level, and then developed through discussion at the NGO forum with government delegations at the conference. One example of this was the 'Women Weaving the World Together' project:

> 'Women Weaving the World Together' was initiated by women in Indonesia, who invited groups of women across the world to create weavings that represented their lives, as a way of sharing life experiences, for the UN conference on women in Beijing. The weavings became a way for women to come together to explore and to discuss experiences, within and between local communities. Participants sewed the weavings together at the NGO Forum where the banner continued to grow and was paraded on the Great Wall of China and at the conference. This process created a powerful experience of transnational linking and solidarity across diverse and common experiences.
>
> (Heerah and Berrios, 1996)

The Global Platform for Action (GPfA), adopted at the UN conference on Women in 1995, claims to offer a powerful agenda for the empowerment of women. It identifies twelve 'critical areas for concern', and related to these, strategic objectives and actions (United Nations, 1995). The GPfA declares its intention to ensure that a gender perspective for the purpose of women's empowerment is reflected in all governmental policies and programmes, and refers to gender mainstreaming as the instrument for achieving this (United Nations, 1995, para 201). It calls on all sectors of civil society and institutions to commit themselves to this aim, and places responsibility on UN organisations to play a key role in monitoring, implementation and follow up government actions.

The GPfA was the outcome of complex and highly contested negotiations between governments and women's organisations, which held widely different concepts of gender equality in relation, for example, to reproductive rights and sexuality[5] (Bunch and Fried, 1996). In this sense, the document illustrates the strengths of gender mainstreaming, and its limitations. These are reflected in the definitions of gender mainstreaming, which focus on the process of integrating gender equality, without defining the content, or referring to contestation within context of local democracy. Definitions offer slightly different interpretations of what is entailed (Squires, 2007). The UN definition is:

> A strategy for making women's as well as men's concerns and experiences an integral dimension of the design, implementation, monitoring and eva-luation of the policies and programmes in all political, economic and societal spheres so that women and men benefit equally and inequality is not perpetuated. The ultimate goal is to achieve gender equality.
>
> (United Nations, 2002, p.2)

The European Commission defines it as:

> The systematic integration of the respective situations, priorities and needs of women and men so women and men in all policies and with a view to promoting equality between men and women and mobilizing all gender policies and measures specifically for the purpose of achieving equality by actively and openly taking into account, at the planning stage, their effects on the respective situation of women and men in implementing monitoring and evaluation.
>
> (Commission of The European Communities 1996, p.2,
> cited in Squires, 2007, p.40)

Both of these definitions aim to make gender equality an integral part of all 'mainstream' public policy making. This was a departure from previous gov-ernmental women's policy agendas arising from the UN Conference on Women in Nairobi, 1985, where the focus and locus of change interventions had been on specific 'women's issues' (Sawer, 1996). The shift of focus from identifying specific women's issues to a requirement to identify the gender impact of all policies was intended to overcome the persistent marginalisation of women's equality. However, its shortcoming is that it does not address resistance to gender equality, and in this respect implies that its integration within organisational processes is unproblematic.

   Gender mainstreaming is open to interpretations stemming from widely differing concepts of gender equality and of the mainstream (Walby, 2011). The dualism between gender equality and mainstream organisational and institutional agendas has led inevitably to a mix of contestation and compromise, which has been analysed within different theoretical vocabularies (see Walby, 2011 for a detailed analysis). A key distinction is between 'integrationalist' and 'transforma-tional' approaches (Rees, 1998; Walby 2011, p.82). Integrationalist approaches introduce a gender perspective within existing policy as a way of more effectively achieving a given policy goal. This might be equivalent to the business case for gender equality. Transformational approaches offer neither assimilation of feminist perspectives into established practice or the maintenance of a dualism between feminist and institutional practice, but a transformation of gender power relations embedded and reproduced in mainstream policy and practice. We continue this discussion further in our analysis of the development of gender equality work in local authorities in Great Britain in the following chapter.

Notes

1 This was extended to four types in Esping-Andersen's *Social Foundations of Postindustrial Economies* (1999).

2 See http://www.forum.awid.org/forum12/2013/02/gross-domestic-product-gdp-growth/ and http://www.stuff.co.nz/business/women-of-influence/8833019/Women-still-waiting-to-be-counted (both accessed 23/6/2014).

3 Brendan Barber, TUC Women's Conference March 2012: http://www.tuc.org.uk/equality/tuc-20764-f0.cfm (accessed 23/6/2014).

4 In the preface to the first edition of *In and Against the State*, the London Edinburgh Weekend Return Group describe themselves as 'a small group of people who work for the state or for organisations who receive money from the state'.

5 See http://www.un.org/womenwatch/daw/beijing15/index.html (accessed 23/6/2014).

3 Dreams and visions of feminist equality in the local state

Introduction

In Chapter 2 we argued that the tension between the coercive and the liberating potential of the welfare state opens up a space for feminist activists to introduce their own agendas for transformative change. Whilst Esping-Andersen (1990) identified an alliance between classes as the only successful way to influence and to extend services provided by welfare states, feminist activists and researchers are concerned with the politics of difference that preclude a simple unified agenda for change. In this chapter we explore the potential and the risks of harnessing the local state to promote gender equality, and argue that feminists must work both 'in and against' the state to influence change. As highlighted in Chapter 2, this is a risky strategy and it has taken on new meaning in recent debates that note the absorption of many feminist demands for equality into neo-liberal agendas, and their mobilization to serve consumerism and higher and different levels of exploitation between women (Eisenstein, 1996, 2009; Fraser, 2009).

We trace the development of gender equality work in local government in Great Britain from the early days of Left Labour administrations in the late 1970s and 1980s up to the legislation that introduced the Gender Equality Duty (GED) in 2008. Although the legislation seemed to promise the next step in gender equality legislation (Fredman, 2001), the context of its implementation was one of prolonged dismantling of the welfare state through radical welfare reforms introduced by Conservative governments in the 1980s and continued by Labour administrations in the 1990s and 2000s. The reforms, carried out in the name of modernisation, have changed the relationship between the state and citizens, the economy and society through the introduction of business processes and privatisation of local services (Clarke and Newman, 1997; Newman and Clarke, 2009).

The British welfare state, as we have come to know it, was established by a Labour government elected in 1945 as a national project of social reconstruction conceived to be part of the post-war settlement. It was designed to reduce social disadvantage through social insurance and public services funded by taxation and based on professional expertise. Dismantling the settlement began in the economic crisis of the mid 1970s, when public spending began to be viewed as an unproductive social cost, rather than a productive collective investment (Johnson, 1990). At the same time social movements challenged the constructs of family, of citizenship and of dependency that were embedded in welfare services and professional expertise. Categories such as race, gender and sexuality that had been perceived to be 'natural' were redefined as socially constructed (Williams, 1989, 1992, 1999). The development of equality work within the local state contributed towards the reworking of these constructs within the modernised welfare state (Newman, 1995, 2002).

Our focus in this chapter is on strategies for promoting and implementing gender equality within local government in Great Britain. The chapter provides the context for our analysis of the Gender Equality Duty and its potential to support transformative change contained in Chapter 5. We begin by briefly reviewing the constructs of gender equality underpinning women's and gender equality practice. We then provide a brief history of the development of gender equality work in local government in Great Britain. This is divided into two phases. The first of these, 1978–97, charts the rise and demise of a brief moment of transformation, sometimes referred to as municipal feminism, that blossomed in the space opened up by the political struggle between the Conservative central government and Labour Party controlled local authorities. The second phase covers the period 1997–2010 and examines what happened to gender equality in local authorities under the modernisation agenda of the 'New Labour' government. The chapter concludes by examining the legislative reforms that resulted in the GED, to frame our discussion of the research findings presented in Chapter 5.

During these periods, as we have shown in Chapter 2, feminist theorisation of the state developed, from being conceived as a unitary or fixed set of structures within which a single set of women's interests were to be represented, towards being a heterogeneous set of relations, within and through which women with different experiences and perspectives were to become political players (London Weekend Return Group, 1979; Watson, 1990). Research accounts of women's and gender equality work within the local state in the early period reflected the double stance held by many women's equality practitioners: being both movement feminist outsiders looking in, and feminist insiders engaging with political processes and organisation structures to create arenas for making change (Itzin and Newman, 1995; Lovenduski and Randall, 1993). This double stance was captured by the term 'in and against the state' (London Weekend Return Group, 1979), which was widely taken up by women's equality practitioners in Great Britain, and is illustrated in the conversations with practitioners of this period in Chapter 4.

In Chapter 2 we highlighted how feminists working in the state have been subject to criticism when becoming too closely associated with 'mainstream' politics. In contrast to these arguments the mainstreaming of equality into political policy and processes was recast as a positive strategy (Rees, 1998, 1999). Once gender mainstreaming was adopted as the preferred strategy within local authorities, the research focus shifted from local democratic political process to discursive constructs of gender rooted in policy and how these might be shaped by practitioners (see, for example, Benschop and Verloo 2006; Eveline and Bacchi, 2005; Nentwich, 2006, Squires, 2005, 2007; Walby, 2005a, 2005b; Woodward, 2003). A consistent thread in feminist research is a concern to identify the factors and conditions for sustaining transformative change as a dimension of a long term political vision of equality against its reduction to short term, limited goals. These debates are considered further below.

Long and short agendas for women's equality: peaks, troughs and streams

Feminist research into the effectiveness of gender equality work within the local state has long been preoccupied with distinctions between liberal and transformational strategies. Research relating to the first decade of equality work critiqued the limited, material outcomes of equal opportunity and diversity policy (Coyle, 1989; Itzin and Newman, 1995; Webb, 1997). In a study of local government and business organisations in the first decades of equal opportunities policy in the 1980s in Great Britain, Cockburn (1989, p.219) problematised the prescriptive nature of much of this research and returned to the question 'what was equal opportunities meant to be?' Referring to Jewson and Mason's (1986) distinction between radical and liberal agendas, she suggested that this dichotomous approach is a 'straightjacket that we need to escape if we are to understand the equal opportunities movement and its potential place in contemporary politics' (Cockburn, 1989, p.215). She supported her argument with an analysis of the diversity and multiplicity of experiences of managers and of employees, illustrating the challenges that equal opportunities can make to the reproduction of power. She concluded that equal opportunity policies may more usefully be understood as being based on a long or a short agenda for change, rather than a liberal/radical opposition (p.218). At its shortest, the agenda is formal and managerial, but nevertheless desirable. At its longest it has to be recognised as a project of transformation of society: 'As such it brings into view the nature and purpose of institutions and the processes by which the power of some groups over others in institutions is built and renewed' (p.218).

Almost a decade later, Rees (1998, 1999) made a similar distinction between equality strategies that are based on longer or shorter agendas for change. Gender mainstreaming, in contrast to equal opportunities, she argued, has the potential to be transformative:

> I have referred to [these] three approaches, equal treatment, positive action and mainstreaming, as tinkering, tailoring and transforming (Rees, 1998). Equal treatment means tinkering with systems to ensure people are treated the same. Positive action means tailoring provision to accommodate difference. People may be treated equally while not being treated the same. Mainstreaming means transformation: it can be defined as integrating equal

opportunities into all systems, structures, actions, policies, programmes and projects – into ways of thinking and doing.

(Rees, 1999, p.27)

In early evaluations of equal opportunities for women, effectiveness was usually taken to refer to structural measures of equality. In later research on gender mainstreaming, 'transformational' was taken to mean dislodging the ways in which gender and equality were constructed within predominant discourses, from a deficit model of disadvantage in which women are a special interest group, to one where women are equally valued. Many of these studies focused on analysing the liberal or transformative constructs of gender that were embedded in the policy process, and how these might be reworked by practitioners (see for example Benschop and Verloo 2006; Eveline and Bacchi, 2005; Squires, 2005, 2007; Walby, 2005a, 2005b; Woodward, 2003). This invited a shift of focus away from externally defined structural measures of inequality, towards an investigation of how power was exercised in the interpretation and implementation of policy (Newman, 2002, 2012; Watson, 1990). While this opened a space for considering how gender relations could be differently constructed by actors within the policy process, it also introduced a new set of risks, and ambiguities. Emphasis on the fluidity of power relations makes it difficult to account for continuity of systematic gender inequality (Webb, 2001; Walby, 2011), and may underestimate the wider contextual factors and political constraints.

Subsequent international research studies have found the impact of gender mainstreaming practice to be uneven, and that its transformative potential is contingent on local political and economic conditions (see, for example, Rees, 2005; Walby, 2005a; Woodward, 2003). While this might be configured as an illustration of how feminist action within the state inevitably leads to co-option or integration, an alternative is to view it more strategically. Rather than as peaks and troughs that suggest a linear progression, we might adopt the metaphor of streams of feminism, each taking up different facets of women's inequality that are configured and reconfigured, both by the social conjuncture and by women's changing political aspirations (Sangster and Luxton, 2013). Newman (2012) introduces the concept of feminist women in the local state 'working the spaces of power' that open up and close down in a fluid landscape of change. This leads us into the substance of the book: to examine the changing politics and underpinning conceptual frameworks and strategies to introduce women's equality within and through the local state in the UK in order to assess their transformational potential and to understand their limitations.

Transformation of gender relations may be variously understood as arriving at an equal valuing of differences between men and women, or as an assertion of equivalence or sameness where gender difference becomes an irrelevance. The implied clarity of the distinction between liberal and transformative strategy casts doubt on the transformative impact of liberal change for many of the individual actors involved. The politics of difference highlighted in Chapter 2 demands that the very notion of transformation is necessarily contested as different ways of understanding gender equality arise, each deeply embedded in the history of feminist, anti-racist and working class social movements (Walby, 2011).

It is often implied that liberal in contrast to transformative strategies amount to co-option of feminist aims within a neo-liberal agenda (see, for example, Eisenstein, 2009; Fraser, 2009). Our research focuses on how their limitations and their transformational potential intermesh with welfare reforms and feminist organisation (Newman, 1995, 2002; Webb, 2001). We investigate in Chapters 4 and 5 how stakeholders in the policy process, including equality practitioners and independent women's organisations, worked the tensions between feminist and 'mainstream' agendas in the context of economic, social and political change (Bacchi and Eveline, 2010; Walby, 2011). We argue that gender equality work in the local state is an unfinished and inevitably contested project in which independent feminist organisations, engaging with the politics of difference, play a crucial role. Equality strategies with long and short agendas, from this perspective, are positioned firmly at the centre of the democratic process.

Phase 1: in and against the state: oppositional politics meets feminist practice: 1978–97

In the first period, beginning in the late 1970s, feminists worked with local Left Labour administrations to defend and extend community based services for women in the context of cutbacks in local government spending and increasing central government control of the powers of the local state (Coote and Campbell, 1982; Goss, 1984). Progressive local Labour administrations were intent on protecting and maintaining collective provision of services and on developing a socialist alternative in opposition to a national Conservative government led by Margaret Thatcher (Boddy and Fudge, 1984). It was a time of widespread industrial action, political turmoil and feminist activism. Gender relations were challenged within the workplace and in domestic and social relations. This was manifest in industrial action and in campaigns for welfare and employment policy to support women's economic independence and autonomy, in campaigns for reproductive rights and against sexual and racist violence. It was in this context of upsurge of Left Labour and feminist activism and economic and social crisis that activists came together in what became an uneasy alliance 'in and against the local state' (London Weekend Return Group, 1979; Coote and Campbell, 1982; Rowbotham *et al.*, 1979/2013). The feminist movement claimed local government as an important site of activity (Coote and Campbell, 1982). One of the first of these was the Women's Rights Working Party initiated by women's groups in the London Borough of Lewisham who demanded that the local authority take an initiative on equal rights for women in 1978 (Goss, 1984). The Working Party was set up with half of its membership drawn from councillors and half from local groups, elected at an open meeting at the Women's Centre. This was followed in spring 1983 by women's committees established in six London Boroughs (ibid.). These developments moved beyond London and, by 1986, 30 local authorities in England had women's committees, many of them initiated by coalitions of independent women's groups, the Labour Party women's section, some elected politicians, and women in trade unions. Lovenduski and Randall (1993, p.151) estimate that, by 1986, 40 per cent of local authorities had some kind of equal opportunities policy covering sex equality and 25 per cent of Labour controlled authorities had women's or equality committees or sub-committees. In some communities, support for women's committees came from local councillors, while in others the initiative came from the women's movement.

Local authorities developed their own forms of socialist renewal, and this was reflected in their equality strategies. In Sheffield, during the 1980s, the focus was primarily on employment, and the economy. A Women's Panel was formed in 1986, and attempts were then made to co-opt members of underrepresented groups of women, and to support local feminist campaigns (Payling, 2014). In Leeds, a conference that drew together Labour Party and SDP women, trade union members, and local women's groups (including Rape Crisis, Asian Women and the 300 Group) resulted in the formation of a women's sub-committee of the Policy and Resources Committee (Flannery and Roelofs, 1984, cited in Gelb, 1989), although many of these were later downgraded or closed by subsequent political administrations.

The following events are selected to offer a sense of the context within which this 'municipal feminism' (Bruegel and Kean, 1995) grew and retreated. The period prior to municipal feminism was marked by significant gains by the feminist movement. In the late 1960s and early 1970s, under a Labour government, public spending on caring services increased its share of all government spending from a quarter to a third (Coote and Campbell, 1982). Much of the additional spending provided state funded alternatives to caring responsibilities previously located in domestic relations within the family and, in doing so, offered women opportunities for paid employment. During this period, feminist campaigns pursued the establishment of equality legislation and resourced support services for women, including independently run refuges for 'battered women'. In 1972 the first Women's Refuge opened and by 1980 there were 200 refuges and a National Women's Aid Federation had been established. The Domestic Violence Act was passed in 1976, establishing women's right to restrain a violent husband or cohabitee. The first Rape Crisis Centre opened in 1976 followed by 15 more in the next five years in different cities. Rape Crisis Centres were instrumental in the formation of campaigns for legislative reform to include marital rape in 1991 in common law and in statute in 1994.[1] In 1975 the National Abortion Campaign was launched and successfully defended the National Abortion Act. In the same year the Equal Pay Act came into force and the Sex Discrimination Act set up the Equal Opportunities Commission with a mandate to oversee implementation of the Equal Pay Act and Sex Discrimination Act. Campaigns for equal rights at work brought feminists into alliance with trade unions and in 1974 a women's rights conference took place at the TUC, organised by the feminist Women's Rights Unit at the National Council for Civil Liberties, and the London Trades Council drew up a ten point Working Women's Charter widely adopted by a network of campaign groups (Coote and Campbell, 1982, p.38). By 1978 a TUC Charter for the Under Fives called for childcare to be available for all children. The Charter was attacked by the Conservative 'party of the family' and the Labour Prime Minister supported the 'need to retain the beneficial influence of the family as a whole' and minimise the 'impact on the family of more mothers going out to work' (ibid., pp.84–85).

Despite Left Labour support for feminist campaigns, the official view of the Labour Party and government remained ambiguous on the status of women (ibid., p.88). In the late 1970s, decisions to cut back public services were presented as an economic necessity, and there were frequent attacks on the inadequacy of public services from the Labour and Conservative right (ibid., p.84). Equality initiatives in local government are often at odds with political leadership in central government, whether Conservative or Labour. However, the conflict was exacerbated when, after a period of widespread public sector strikes in response to the Labour government's attempts to impose a wage freeze, a Conservative government was elected in 1979, led by Margaret Thatcher, the first woman prime minister of Great Britain. Their manifesto commitment was to roll back the state, reduce the power of trade unions and privatise public services. Conservative governments were re-elected in 1983, 1987 and 1992, remaining in power until 1997.

Coote and Campbell (1982, p.93) succinctly summarise the feminist transformational agenda for UK public services in the 1980s:

> The women's liberation movement is engaged in a three way struggle: to defend state services and benefits, in their present imperfect condition, against governments committed to public expenditure cuts; to transform the assumptions and rules that govern them, and radically improve their quality; and to win new gains in the form of additional benefits and services, as well as state funding for independent feminist initiatives … The fight against public spending cuts, led by trade unions, focused on jobs. Feminists attempted to insert a new dimension to the campaigns involving a critique of services and proposals to change them. This was the substance of feminist initiatives to engage with Left Labour authorities, 'in and against' the local state.

An important milestone for feminist activity during this period was the formation of the GLC[2] Women's Committee in 1982, the first full local government women's committee to be established. Formed at an open meeting attended by over 60 organisations and a spread of political opinion, the Committee recruited between 70 and 90 staff to work in a Support Unit, including movement activists, experienced trade unionists and others with no activist background. The Committee set out to improve employment conditions for women, services for women and girls and their political representation. This was done by direct funding of independent projects, but also by subsidised training and education targeted towards women in specific disadvantaged groups. In its first four years, the Committee awarded £30m in grants to childcare, health, women's refuges, resource centres, information and advice, and counselling for women (Coote and Campbell, 1982). Nine service-based working groups and eight women, including black and minority ethnic, lesbian and trade union women, were elected to the committee. Calls were made by feminists for similar committees in London Boroughs and 14 London local authorities set up women's committees in the 1980s with dedicated women's support units at some stage (Goss, 1984; Labour Research Department, 1995; Roleoffs, 1983).

This transformational project came under serious attack when, in 1983, a Conservative government was re-elected with a manifesto commitment to abolish the GLC and five other metropolitan councils on the grounds of fiscal irresponsibility, being politically out of step and funding alternative lifestyles that were part of an immoral attempt to undermine the family (Bashevkin, 2007, p.56). Education and housing services began to be removed from local authority control and local authorities were required, under the process of compulsory competitive tendering (CCT), to seek the privatisation of services they had formerly run. Central government funding was reduced and controls were placed on the abilities of local authorities to raise revenue. Inevitably public services were reduced. State subsidised childcare, school meals, and residential care for the elderly and people with disabilities, and health services were the hardest hit, reducing women's employment and services on which many relied, usually the poorest women with intersecting equality disadvantage (Escott and Whitfield, 1995).

In 1986 the Conservative government succeeded in abolishing the GLC. This brought a significant loss of funding to local and national women's organisations, loss of direct political representation of women in planning and resource allocation, and loss of strategic focus on equality throughout London (Bashevkin, 2007, p.55). The GLC was later replaced by the Greater London Authority (GLA), with a much reduced strategic function, but which, under Left Labour leadership, continued to promote a London-wide feminist strategic policy agenda (see Chapter 4). Another significant attack on equalities in local government service provision came with the infamous Section 28 of the Local Government Act 1988, which outlawed promotion of homosexuality in schools. Section 28 was inserted into the Local Government Act in direct response to the production of a resource guide for teachers in London schools with 'positive images' of lesbians and gay men. The wording of the Act stated:

> A local authority shall not intentionally promote homosexuality or publish material with the intention of promoting homosexuality; a local authority shall not promote the teaching in any maintained school of the acceptability of homosexuality as a pretended family relationship.
>
> (Section 28, Local Government Act, 1988)

Local campaigners lobbied Labour local authorities to defy the law and women's equality units came under additional public scrutiny (Gelb, 1989). Divisions opened up within the Labour Party and on Women's Committees, with some prepared to defend programmes of work with lesbians, whilst some preferred to prioritise less contentious issues. (See Chapter 4 for illustrations.)

During this time there were constant media attacks on Labour local administrations with progressive equalities policies singled out as the 'Loony Left'. The media and Conservative Party attacks targeted local authorities, particularly London Boroughs that supported the feminist agenda, as wasting public money on marginal groups who lived outside normal family values. Fearing electoral defeat, even Left Labour councils began to retreat from the gains made in the early 1980s. By 1995 only four full Women's Committees remained in London (Islington, Southwark, Greenwich and Waltham Forest); and 10 women's sub-committees (Labour Research Department, 1995). Of the four, two were cut and the remaining two merged within Policy or Social Justice Units. The three main reasons for decline of Women's Committees were financial reductions, changes in political control and devolved powers to departments including equality mainstreaming. Councils under pressure tended to merge separate women's, disability, race and lesbian and gay units and reduce the number of staff. Others were merged into generic policy units, social justice or social exclusion units. Alongside this, it was felt more effective to devolve equalities work within departments. Often this was accompanied by a massive cut in resources for women's equality work and reduced quality of service for women (Labour Research Department, 1995).

Despite its relative transience, the early part of this period represents perhaps the closest glimpse of what a feminist transformational agenda might look like. In the following section we consider these events in relation to the concept of 'municipal feminism'. This is followed, in Chapter 4, with recollections and reflections on these events in conversation with equality practitioners of this period.

Theorising practice: the rise and demise of municipal feminism

Following Lovenduski and Randall (1993), Bruegel and Kean (1995) take municipal feminism as a label to examine the links and differences between municipal socialism and feminism and to distinguish it from liberal equal rights feminism and earlier Marxist and radical feminism. Its distinctiveness was its emphasis on the public sector as a potential instrument of wider change, a concern with the inequalities between women as well as between men and women and the potential for a liberating welfare state. Bruegel and Kean (1995) identify 1983–87 as a specific historical moment when Labour political agendas and socialist feminist goals converged. This convergence took place at local level, within Labour councils in opposition to a Conservative national administration. Municipal feminism of the 1980s, they argue, drew on the women's movement of the 1970s and the extra parliamentary Left. Rather than accepting institutions of the state uncritically as mechanisms for change, municipal feminism recognised bureaucracies as 'structures of semi-autonomous, gendered power', and in this sense broke with 'welfarism' in emphasising the need to reconfigure the operational processes of the local state as well as to get policies formally adopted:

> Like municipal socialism it [municipal feminism] sought to use the existing institutions of the state for new ends. But it sought to go further, to recast the way the state operated and to take on the institutions of the labour movement.
>
> (Bruegel and Kean, 1995, p.149)

Central to it was the concept of a state that could be feminised and remoulded to regulate the market more, but only by working in and against it. To this end, equality advisors were often recruited from the women's movement to staff women's units and committees (Cockburn, 1989; Goss, 1984). Often they had little experience of working in local authorities and had to learn to become effective within political and bureaucratic structures and processes to build credibility with experienced civil servants. Treading a thin line between being answerable to senior managers and politicians and a resource for external constituencies, women and/or ethnic minorities, the disabled or lesbian and gay communities, these jobs both attracted progressives and threatened to destroy them (Cockburn, 1989, p.218). This experience of negotiating conflicting accountabilities and loyalties is explored in the accounts of women's equality practitioners in Chapters 4 and 5.

From the outset explicit connections were made between feminist and democratic local politics. The GLC began its programme with a series of open meetings, conferences, co-options and other consultation exercises designed to bring local women, particularly those who are under-represented in the democratic process, into decision making (Gelb, 1989). As Thobani (1995, p.153) noted:

> Until recently, most of the decision making meetings in local government would have been all white and mainly men. Millions of pounds worth of services serve particular sections of the community while ignoring the needs of others. Services mirror the values of the people who provide them and embody the values of those who manage them. Where groups that experience discrimination get services the provision is often paternalistic, patronising or culturally inappropriate.

Attempting to address these issues constituted a political challenge to established patterns in local authorities, labour movement and party politics, bringing the politics of difference to the forefront of local democratic structures. The alliance did not mean that feminists were pushing on an open door. The local Labour Party establishment was often hostile to the development of Women's Committees, which were caught up in the power struggles between the old guard right, the hard left and the centre or soft left in the Labour Party of the 1980s.

In terms of Cockburn's (1989, 1991) distinction between the long and the short agendas, the agenda was long. Its aim was to do more than help individuals move up the hierarchy (1991, p.148), but rather was concerned to flatten hierarchies and to give women from different backgrounds a voice (Goss, 1984). It had its roots in a number of traditions, including earlier labourist municipal feminism. During this early period, democratisation of some local Labour administrations was extended by the devolution of power to local communities and alliances with trade unions and community organisations (Bruegel and Kean, 1995; Newman, 1995; Scott, 2002; Thobani, 1995). The advance of women's equality was an explicitly political project, aiming to transform how women live their lives by challenging power relations between men and women at home as well as at work.

Municipal feminism captures the experience of a brief window of time in the 1980s and early 1990s when shared purpose was constructed by key actors who had come together with a long agenda for change, in the context of socialist and feminist political struggle. Their agenda was hammered out despite media hostility and attack from central government bent on reducing the power of local government and marketising the local state. The project was precarious and vulnerable to the changing whims and fortunes of key players within the Labour Party and to the difficulties of overcoming institutionalised male resistance to change (Cockburn, 1991; Coyle, 1989; Goss, 1984; Webb, 1997). In this it shared many of the features of femocracy, where effectiveness at national level was dependent on sustaining its roots in the feminist movement, while making the necessary compromises to forge an alliance with the political administration in power. Bruegel and Kean (1995) argue that the features of municipal feminism, despite its limitations, demonstrate the transformative dimension and potential of equalities work in and around local government. This potential was developed in response to the limited prospects for central government action on equality, following the Conservative Party victory in 1979.

As the Labour Party distanced itself from 'old Labour', particularly radical Left Labour politics, and adopted the politics of the 'third way', many left wing councils shifted from radical to conservative ends of the political spectrum (Cockburn, 1991). Women's employment conditions deteriorated as services were cut and outsourced (Coote and Campbell, 1982; Escott and Whitfield, 1995; Webb, 2001). The moment of municipal feminism ended and the limited gains achieved can be associated with the assault on local government, the new realist accommodation with the market and the slimming down of equal opportunities after 1987 (Cockburn, 1991). The refusal of the 'New Labour' government to distance itself from 'family values' and the gendered division of labour within it, despite feminist work to embed feminist vision of change within their agenda for modernisation, severely undermined the transformational dimension of the feminist equality project and of their Left Labour allies (Coote and Campbell, 1982; Coote, 2000).

Although the transformational potential of municipal feminism and the alliance between Left Labour politicians was short-lived, one of its legacies extends beyond local and national politics. The development of transnational feminist activism has embedded women's rights in supranational bodies such as the UN, EU and Council of Europe. This remains a central feature of the gender equality framework in the UK, and has provided instruments for local activists and opportunities to build partnerships and networks for promoting equality within the local state. Before moving on to examine the second phase of women's equality in local government, the following section examines how these links were made and have survived in less hospitable times.

Linking local and transnational feminist activism

Transnational feminist activity, highlighted in Chapter 2, became a lifeline for municipal feminists struggling to hold on to the progress made in the 1980s. Within the UK, EU funded programmes produced a wealth of transnational feminist projects, sponsored and part-funded by local government and based on international partnerships (Walby, 2011; Rees, 1998). These transnational partnerships played an important role in inspiring breadth of vision beyond local and national boundaries and boosting the profile and influence of local groups through accessing policy makers and resources (Page, 1997, 2003). Women's equality work in and with local authorities gained a national and international policy profile, which often increased its credibility and local influence. Local authority take up of transnational partnership opportunities depended on the initiative of individuals who saw international linking as a catalyst for local women's equality activism. One such initiative was the 'Time of Our Lives' project, a transnational EU funded partnership with a local authority in the South West of England, led by the Trades Union Congress, to develop flexible working hours to benefit employees and service users (TUC, 2001). Another local authority partnership initiative is considered in Box 3.1.

Box 3.1: Transnational feminism: from the local to the global

In 1992, an equality advisor in London Borough of Lewisham obtained EU funding for a project linking older women's organisations in the Italian commune of Perugia and in her local authority. Through transnational visits and joint events links developed between older women in a variety of local ethnic minority communities in Lewisham and they became active in local pensioner lobbies and local authority policy forums. A joint delegation travelled to Beijing in 1995 to take part in the older women's caucus at the Fourth World UN conference on Women and in the NGO Forum (Page, 1997). Following this, the European network 'Own Europe' was formed, whose members have subsequently been delegates at CEDAW conferences and lobbied to ensure gender issues are addressed within country reports on changing demographics and services for pensioners (see, for example, Sclater, 2012).

In 1997, a successful bid was made to the EU Fourth Action Programme for a partnership project to develop gender mainstreaming. Partner organisations were a national Italian trade union for public service workers, a centre for the unemployed in Dublin, Ireland, and a network of neighbourhood councils in the Netherlands and the London Borough. The partners developed an action learning methodology for gender mainstreaming, and wrote case studies of how this approach had enabled them to develop local participative projects to promote women's equality within their local context. Partners stated that their transnational learning had supported and enabled development of their local work, raising its status and profile. Within the local authority, the transnational links established by the lead equality advisor broadened local horizons and lent political status, financial resource and greater credibility and profile to gender equality work (Page, 2003).

In preparation for the UN 4th World Conference on Women in 1995, mechanisms were established for feminist organisations to work with UK government delegations to put together position statements for negotiation at regional preparatory meetings and at the conference itself. Ongoing briefings and consultations on the final text of the Global Platform for Action (GPfA) were organised at the UN conference and parallel NGO forum. NAWO,[3] an independent feminist umbrella organisation, and the Women's National Commission,[4] each played key roles in promoting participation in this process. These events were a catalyst for feminists from a wide variety of organisations and constituencies to come together across the political spectrum, often for the first time. These were rare opportunities for senior civil servants, trade unions and national feminist campaigns to work together, drafting and negotiating the final text of the Global Platform for Action, the international benchmarking standard for gender equality that would be adopted by governments at the conference. For equality advisors in some local authorities, the experience of forming collaborations and of the negotiating process added political credibility to local gender mainstreaming initiatives and leverage for broadening women's participation in local policy processes (Page, 1997).

Gender mainstreaming, first adopted in the GPfA in 1995, was endorsed in 1997 at the Treaty of Amsterdam and became the official policy approach to gender equality in the European Union. It was then taken up by the EU member states and adopted as a criterion within EU structural funding programmes and throughout EU policy processes. UK Conservative governments (1979–97) had ignored previous UN protocols concerning gender sensitive policy machinery, and refused to sign the 1992 Maastricht treaty, which included a Social Charter with important ramifications for women. While the Conservative government signed up to the principle of gender mainstreaming in successive international arenas, including the GPfA in 1995 (United Nations, 1995), implementation within the UK was slow. Following election of the Labour government in 1997, feminist strategy sought to embed equality in government using gender mainstreaming in the context of a push to modernise Labour Party policy (Coote, 2000). However, in 2005 the senior civil servant who chaired the Women's National Commission observed that while there had been limited thinking within government about either the exact aims of gender mainstreaming or the means whereby it might be achieved, it did have a significant effect on local as well as national governmental strategy to promote women's equality (Veitch, 2005).

Phase 2: from political project to business case: gender equality and New Labour: 1997–2010

Leading up to the 1997 election of a 'New Labour' government, led by Tony Blair, feminists sought to embed a women's equality lens within measures to modernise the local state (Breitenbach *et al.*, 2002; Newman, 2002). This period is characterised by the introduction of business principles into the governance of public services, extending the modernisation programme introduced by the Conservative government. During this period, 'gender equality' replaced 'women's equality', and generic equality teams often replaced strand specific equality advisors.

Tony Blair's explicit project was one of modernisation of the Labour Party and its manifesto, with the intention of removing the last traces of socialism. The combination of a 'modernised' Labour Party and the feeling that Conservative neo-liberalism had run out of steam did contribute to a change of government in 1997. Feminist women within the Labour Party played a leading role in shaping the modernisation project, to address gender equality in social policy and in gender relations. Female voters had been identified as key constituents in the election campaign, and women-only shortlists were adopted in selected constituencies. An unprecedented 101 female MPs were elected, on a wave of celebration and anticipation following the long years of austerity under Conservative administrations. However, this was swiftly followed by disillusionment. The government set about disowning the politically driven agendas of 'old Labour', in favour of a 'third way' that attempted a fusion of neo-liberal economic policy with social inclusion and citizen participation (Clarke and Newman, 1997) but which did not embrace a redistribution of gender power in families or institutions (Coote, 2000; Williams, 1999). The media lost no time in naming the newly elected MPs 'Blair's babes', creating a group portrait of smiling women wearing jewel coloured suits that had been stipulated for media coverage, eagerly clustered around a jubilant Tony Blair (Ward, 2000, p.23). This became the touchstone for almost every collective profile of Labour women, and indeed as Harriet Harman, the first Minister for Women commented:

> I warned No 10 that we would look like sheep and he (Blair) the only ram … they said I was being prima donna-ish.
>
> (cited in Ward, 2000, p.23)

After the 1997 election of a Labour government, women MPs and Labour activists associated with the campaign reflected on the bitter battles that ensued, and the difficulty of maintaining a collective feminist stance in the face of punitive Party discipline and pejorative media scrutiny (Coote, 2000). As one of them observed, never had so relatively few politicians been called so many names over so many newspaper columns in so short a time (Ward, 2000, p.23). It became apparent that the commitment of the New Labour government to promoting women's access to government and to gender balance in parliament was effectively part of the smoke screen that obscured continuity in neo-liberal reform. The reforms of public services extended those introduced by the Conservative government and embraced many of the features of the managerial state that would subsequently be taken up in public services throughout the European Union. These included the introduction of market mechanisms and contracts, the privatisation of some public bodies and services, and the incursion of business values into public management, transforming the relationship between state and public (Clarke and Newman, 1997; Newman and Clarke, 2009). Radical changes were introduced in successive waves of reform driven by central governments throughout this period, and during the period of our research into the implementation of the GED in 2008. Restructuring altered the internal organisation and governance of public authorities, changing the role of elected local politicians, managers and equality advisors and their relation to citizens and service users. As public services were increasingly commissioned and delivered through inter-organisational partnerships and business processes, the scope of local government equality policy and practice extended beyond the confines of local government into commissioning and contracting with other public, independent and private sector organisations (Newman and Clarke, 2009). As Chapter 5 illustrates, while this provided scope for some managers to promote gender equality, new challenges were introduced by the growing complexity of internal and external organisational relationships, the imperative to demonstrate a business case and to meet centrally defined performance targets alongside citizen and service user expectations.

In an edited volume Breitenbach *et al.* (2002) analyse the changing politics of equalities work in local government in the period leading up to the election of the Labour government in 1997. As New Labour gained influence in local political administrations during the 1990s, managerialism, a cornerstone of its policy, took hold. Women's Units adapted to the times:

> We couched our work in the dominant language of the council and sought to position women in debates and arguments in ways such as to result in maximum political effect and practical outcomes. ... We would map our understandings against the emerging priorities, concepts and explanations that shape mainstream local government policy. ... We looked for ways the agenda we pursued with and for women might be interpolated into the council's agenda.
>
> (Scott, 2002, p.168)

Newman (1995, 2002) argued that the push for business efficiency first introduced in the late 1980s by Margaret Thatcher's Conservative government continued to gather momentum in the 1990s and, under New Labour, did help to legitimise a concern for equal opportunities, while also robbing it of its political effectiveness. A new concept of 'managing diversity' was introduced alongside 'equal opportunity'. In contrast to equal opportunities in which equality groups are constructed through a discourse of deficit, diversity is reframed as a positive business asset (Newman, 2002; Wrench, 2005). Some members of equality groups welcomed this change of approach, in which they became a valued resource, rather than embodying disadvantage. A positive result of the business case was to increase the numbers of women at senior level, through local and national business initiatives such as Opportunities 2000 (Kettle, 1998), and as a result of 'Best Value', a national standard linked to government funding for local authority services. However the performance demands of the business culture marginalised equality issues unless they could be coupled to other sets of goals.

This major change in the rationale for doing equality work was introduced within local Labour authorities, leading up to the general election, through changes in resourcing and governance of public services. Local authority regulatory and support bodies developed benchmarking systems that incorporated the business case and introduced reward systems based on achievement of approved standards. Towards the end of the 1990s, a group of feminist and anti-racist equality consultants, many of whom were former equalities advisors in local government, developed systems for benchmarking that were adopted in 2001 as the Equality Standard for Local Government, and then from 2009 the Equality Framework.[5] Nationally, this process was led and resourced from the Local Government Improvement and Development Agency (IDeA),[6] which provided funds for some local authorities to bring in equality consultants to raise their standard and improve their performance. By the end of this second phase of gender equality work, many former equality advisors, who had previously been directly employed, were acting as independent consultants to local authorities and public service organisations to put systems in place for compliance with equality legislation and to achieve a higher standard in equality benchmarking (see Chapter 4). The Equality Standard, especially, was deemed to be a valuable lever to promote equality as it was tied to national performance targets for resource allocation to local government. Benchmarking frameworks proved invaluable for enabling smaller and less experienced local authorities to achieve compliance and to raise their standards, putting processes in place to embed gender and other equality strands into management processes, and training managers to implement equality impact assessments (Chapters 4 and 5).

During the introduction of these changes in the late 1990s and early 2000s, many of the women and men who subscribed to elements of municipal feminism had to distance themselves sharply from past associations, and translate their values into the accepted rhetoric of business benefits of diversity in management and of service quality. While more women had moved into senior management, inequalities in pay between women had widened (Webb, 2001). However, it was also the case that many of the women who did move into senior management exercised power in ways designed to lead gender culture change, and to engage women in the project of democratising local government, often at considerable cost to themselves (Maddock, 1999). As we demonstrate in Chapter 5, while the increasing presence of women at senior level was frequently taken as evidence that women's equality had been achieved, it was the presence of a transformational vision of gender equality, linked to independent activism, that was the crucial factor in protecting and promoting the gender equality agenda.

These changes continue to have a major and contradictory impact on how equality agendas are played out in local government (Newman, 2002). The predominant rationale for equality work was no longer primarily based on a political vision of redistributive justice and equality, but overlaid by a business case for 'fairness' implemented through legislative compliance, performance targets and benchmarking for quality assurance. In the period that followed, further discursive shifts occurred. Human rights and social inclusion were introduced through EU legislation and directives. A single equalities body, the Equality and Human Rights Commission (EHRC), replaced the three commissions responsible for overseeing compliance on gender, race and disability equality. These discursive shifts were taken up locally in operational strategies that introduced new opportunities and constraints. In Chapter 5 we explore how equalities practitioners engaged with these changes. In the following section we turn to an analysis of legislative innovation that underpinned strategic change in gender equality practice at local level.

Rethinking equality legislation: harnessing the coercive power of the state?

By the 1990s benchmarking and performance management had become favoured strategies for operationalising equality in local government. However, performance based initiatives such as the Equality Standard were argued by some to have a limited impact because they lacked strong enforcement mechanisms (see O'Cinneide, 2004). By the second administration of New Labour (2001–5) greater scrutiny was placed on the effectiveness of the equality legislation in tackling inequality in public service delivery. Prior to the Equality Act 2010, most of the equality legislation in the UK was applied without distinction to both public and private sector organisations and employers. Most equality legislation, then and now, takes a reactive approach, which provides rights of redress for victims of discrimination.

By the end of the 1990s there was widespread agreement that the law had reached the limits of its usefulness in reducing discrimination and inequality. Much of the existing anti-discrimination legislation was based on employment law and was considered less effective in confronting discrimination in service provision (O'Cinneide, 2004). There were early attempts to model specific legislation in the public sector that crossed equality strands and which covered the delivery of public services as well as employment. The legislation took the form of 'duties' imposed on regional administrations to pursue equality issues beyond the existing anti-discrimination legislation. Section 75 of the Northern Ireland Act 1998 imposed equality duties on a wide range of Northern Irish authorities whilst s.120 of the Wales Act 1998 imposed a similar duty on the Welsh Assembly. In Scotland there was a weaker set of 'enabling powers' to promote equal opportunities (see O'Cinneide, 2004, pp.52–59). Interestingly, in England the test bed for a cross-strand public sector equality duty was the Greater London Authority (GLA). Section 33 of the Greater London Authority Act 1999 introduced an equality duty that required the Mayor and the Greater London Assembly to have 'due regard to the principle that there should be equality of opportunity for all people' (s.33(1)). This, of course, stood in direct contradiction to section 28 of the Local Government Act 1988, although section 28 was not formally repealed until 2003.[7]

The impetus to extend and strengthen these early attempts to formalise and regulate equality in the public sector followed the Stephen Lawrence inquiry, which uncovered serious institutionalised race discrimination in the Metropolitan Police Force.[8] After the MacPherson Report that followed the inquiry, there was recognition that the law needed to take a different approach to challenging institutional discrimination in public services. In a review of the equality legislation, Hepple *et al.* (2000) provided 53 detailed recommendations about how change could be achieved. Their leading claim was that 'the present framework places too much emphasis on state regulation and too little on the responsibility of organisations and individuals to generate change' (p.xiii). Their recommendations for change included the public sector taking a lead via the introduction of positive duties to promote equality and for a process of negotiated change within public authorities.

Reflecting the seriousness of the Stephen Lawrence inquiry, the first of these duties, the Race Equality Duty, was introduced in 2001 under the Race Relations (amendment) Act 2000. The second duty to be introduced was the Disability Equality Duty in December 2006 as part of the Disability Discrimination Act 2005 and the final duty, the Gender Equality Duty, came into force in April 2007 as part of the Equality Act 2006. These separate equality duties were combined with five other 'protected characteristics', derived from EU Directives (age, religion or belief, sexual orientation, pregnancy and maternity, gender reassignment) to form a single Public Sector Equality Duty in the Equality Act 2010.

It is worth noting here that there was a five year gap between the Race Equality Duty and the duties on disability and gender. The positive duties for disability and gender were won by the determination of equality activists both outside and within government. The disability lobby in the UK was active and vocal in its attempts to establish a legal duty for disabled people in public bodies (Sayce and O'Brien, 2004). In relation to gender, the Equal Opportunities Commission (EOC) and the Fawcett Society were instrumental in pushing the government to fulfil its promise to extend a public sector duty to gender.[9] Interestingly, the EOC were keen that a duty should cover women's concerns in relation to public service delivery and the Fawcett Society, at that time, was particularly concerned that a gender duty should address women's treatment in the criminal justice system.[10] As Chapter 4 shows, feminist activists were working hard within local government to implement the existing duty in the GLA and to extend this beyond London.

The most important point to note about the Public Sector Equality Duties is that they were unlike any previous equality legislation in that they did not provide additional rights for individuals but rather placed responsibilities on public authorities as employers and service providers. In this respect they were considered to be a positive, proactive approach to equality that did not depend on discrimination having already taken place. They were designed to directly change organisational behaviour rather than provide a rights-based approach that simply punishes transgressors without necessarily effecting wider change (Bell, 2010). They did not replace the existing equality legislation, which still provides legal remedies for individuals who have suffered discrimination. Rather they sought to pre-empt legal cases by requiring public authorities to anticipate and address potential sources of discrimination before cases emerged. McCrudden (2007, p.259) noted that this change in approach adopted principles of reflexive regulation discussed in Chapter 1, where 'the trick ... is for the legal system to construct a set of procedural stimuli that lead to the targeted subsystem adapting itself'. Another key feature of proactive legislation is that enforcement is, in the first instance, considered to be prompted by the groups it is designed to protect or, using a term favoured by New Labour politicians, 'stakeholders'. By seeking a consultative, inclusive approach to changing institutions, the principles underpinning the Public Sector Equality Duty seemed to have some resonance with Cockburn's (1989, 1991) arguments for a transformational 'long agenda' for pursuing equality. It is also clear that, by inviting stakeholder involvement, they redistributed power (Nonet and Selznick, 1978/2001) and provided the potential for equality activists to harness the coercive power of the state.

The legal mechanism that breathes life into the duties is the requirement for public authorities to have 'due regard' in all of their public functions to eliminate unlawful discrimination and harassment and to promote good relations and equality of opportunity. In practice this approach was designed to ensure the mainstreaming of equality issues and to counter criticisms that equal opportunities were confined to politically driven initiatives by specialist advisors and senior management and were not 'owned' by the managers responsible for putting them into practice (Rees, 1998, 1999). In some respects this attempt to require integration of equalities promotion into management processes and practices addressed some of the issues articulated by Jewson and Mason (1986) that had been long identified by equalities researchers and activists, that the greatest block to putting equality policies into practice is often the disassociation between the levels at which equality policy is formed and where it needs to be operationalised (see also Bacchi and Eveline, 2010).

The organisational mechanism that demonstrated 'due regard' and which required the engagement of operational managers was a process of Equality Impact Assessment (EIA) on all of the proposed and current activities of the authority with the aim of ensuring that people with 'protected characteristics' from each of the legally identified equality strands were not disadvantaged (Conley and Page, 2010). This process was not new but mainstreamed a function that had previously been viewed as a specialist concern, located with equalities advisors, identifying it instead as a management responsibility. Where a service identified a potential unequal impact on access or provision of services, in employment, or any aspect of resource allocation or decision making, it should give due regard to modify the policy or practice (EOC, 2006). Whilst never specifically required by the legislation, the absence or inadequacy of EIAs has been and continues to be a key feature in the enforcement of the equality duties, forming the basis of a number of the cases taken to judicial review by external stakeholders (Bell, 2010; Fredman, 2011; Conley, 2012a).

All of the duties adopted a similar format with a set of substantive 'general duties' placed on public authorities to eliminate unlawful discrimination and harassment and to promote equality of opportunity. Each equality duty also contained a set of more 'specific duties' which were procedural requirements in relation to the disadvantaged groups covered in each of the pieces of legislation. The duty to consult with members of the relevant protected groups was contained in the specific duties. It is important to note at this point that the focus on participation increased with each successive equality duty. In the Race Equality Duty, the specific duties included an 'expectation' that groups affected by their policies and their provisions to meet the duty would be consulted. There was a strong emphasis in the Disability Equality Duty on involvement of people with disabilities and there was an express requirement to do so in the specific duties. However, the focus was on direct participation rather than collective representation. In the Gender Equality Duty (GED), the specific duties required that public authorities consult stakeholders and their collectives, including trade unions, and take into account their views in formulating gender equality objectives.

These conceptual differences in the equality law provided an important opportunity for equality activists to strengthen their bargaining position, considered in more detail in Chapter 5. However, although the Public Sector Equality Duties were undoubtedly a breakthrough in the reconceptualisation of equality law in the UK there has been a mixed response to their effectiveness (Bell, 2010; Conley and Page, 2010; Fredman, 2011). Early assessment of the first positive equality duty on race found that engagement with the legislation was variable, particularly in relation to progress on employment related issues (Equal Opportunities Review, 2002). The Audit Commission (2004) similarly found an implementation gap between policy and outcomes, whilst O'Cinneide (2004) argued the underlying problem was a weakness in the enforcement mechanisms. Inconsistency in the quality of EIAs has been a major concern, with criticisms from a wide range of commentators, academic and practitioner, that they are easily construed as a bureaucratic hurdle and a 'tick box exercise' (see Chapter 5). Again these criticisms have some resonance with Jewson and Mason's (1986) finding that the impact of equality policy can be undermined by resentful or simply over-worked public sector managers charged with their execution. Much of this criticism was levelled at the Race Equality Duty, the first of the duties. In contrast, the Disability Equality Duty introduced a statutory requirement to consult which has been taken up by independent activists, and led to significant successful legal challenge.

Introduced five years after the Race Equality Duty, the GED was considerably more developed. Although it had only been in existence for six months before the Equality Bill was announced, it would be subsumed into a single equality duty in what became the Equality Act 2010. In this brief window of opportunity, although often poorly drafted, EIAs had proven to be valuable tools for equality actors to encourage service delivery teams to engage with gender equality issues in local government (Conley and Page, 2010). These are issues that we elaborate in Chapters 5 and 6.

The Equality Act 2010

On the last page of the 2005 Labour Party Manifesto, a pledge was made to introduce a Single Equality Act to 'simplify' and 'modernise' 40 years of complex equality legislation during the 2005–10 parliament. Following the re-election of a Labour government, the Discrimination Law Review (DLR) was established to work towards this goal, oversee the consultation process and set in motion the parliamentary process for the new legislation. In addition, an Equalities Review was commissioned by the government to provide an independent assessment. The remit of the Equalities Review was far broader than the legal focus of the DLR and its aims were to:

Provide an understanding of the long term and underlying causes of disadvantage that need to be addressed by public policy

Make practical recommendations on key policy priorities for: the Government and public sector; employers and trade unions; civic society and the voluntary sector

Inform both the modernisation of equality legislation, towards a Single Equality Act; and the development of the new Commission for Equality and Human Rights.

(Equalities Review, 2007, p.13)

The final report of the Equalities Review was published in February 2007. In line with its remit, the report was broad ranging, recommending more integrated implementation strategies across equalities areas including the adoption of a single public sector equality duty. The report was quite candid and in the foreword the chair of the Review Panel, Trevor Philips, states:

A few of our conclusions may be less readily embraced by some, as we have tried to resist the temptation to anticipate criticism and adjust our findings to avoid it. We believe that equality is too important for timidity and half measures.

(Equalities Review, 2007, p.4)

It was therefore disappointing that the DLR consultation paper released in June 2007, putting forward proposals for a Single Equality Act, took an unambitious approach that sought to maintain the *status quo* in relation to older discrimination legislation (Discrimination Law Review, 2007). Most notably, the ensuing Green Paper was silent in relation to some important principles established in the existing Public Sector Equality Duties such as involvement of stakeholders, the requirement to set equality objectives, the requirement for impact assessments and the duty to consult with trade unions.

The consultation process that accompanied the Green Paper revealed a great deal of disappointment with the proposals, and criticism of the Green Paper obviously elicited some concern on behalf of the Government. Extensive debate had taken place within the consultation on the DLR about the advantages and risks of merging the single duties. There was a general consensus that a single duty would more easily allow policy to cut across equality strands, in order to address intersections of inequality. However evidence was submitted by a wide range of bodies, including the EOC, CRE and DRC, in which strong concerns were expressed about the potential loss of single strands, and in particular the gender equality strand. As a result of these concerns, and extensive lobbying by equality organisations, the Single Equality Act, due to be announced in the Queen's speech in November 2007, was withdrawn until 2008. The White Paper, *The Equality Bill – Government Response to the Consultation*, was published on 21 July 2008.

Between the publication of the Green Paper and the White Paper, Cabinet responsibility for the Equality Bill passed from Ruth Kelly to Harriet Harman. This change of leadership proved significant, as the White Paper contained some innovations to the equality legislation. Harriet Harman introduced a new public sector socio-economic duty, which required public authorities 'to consider how their decisions might help to reduce the inequalities associated with socio-economic disadvantage'.[11] Other innovations included an extension to permitted positive action in the recruitment and selection of employees, allowing employers for the first time to make voluntary recruitment decisions based on protected character-istics where this would improve the representation of disadvantaged groups in the workplace. The Bill also contained provisions that would allow discrimination claims which combine two protected characteristics, rather than making separate claims. In relation to equal pay the Bill contained provisions for mandatory equal pay audits in workplaces with 250 or more employees.

The passage of the Bill through parliament and the House of Lords was heavily contested by the Conservative Party in opposition. For a while it was feared that it would not be passed before the 2010 general election and was at risk of being abandoned if the Conservatives won. The Equality Act finally made it on to the Statute books on 8 April 2010 – a month before the general election that resulted in the election of a Conservative–Liberal Democrat coalition govern-ment. It soon became clear that the passage of the Act was not completely held up by the Conservatives because much of its content, certainly on any of the innovative aspects, was subject to secondary legislation, including the specific duties for the single public sector equality duty. The Act included only the provisions for the general duties and as such was rather vague on detail. The provision for specific duties, the element of the legislation that provides the concrete procedural requirements, depended on secondary legislation giving Ministers of the Crown powers to impose specific duties on public authorities at a later date. The powers were devolved to the Scottish Parliament and the Welsh Assembly.

The results of the consultation published in a policy statement (GEO, 2011) make interesting reading. The document highlights that there was considerable disagreement on the form the specific duties should follow, with public sector employers' bodies on the whole requiring less prescription, whilst stakeholder groups required greater or equivalent levels of prescription to that contained in the existing specific duties for race, gender and disability. After a twice extended consultation process the regulations for the specific duties in England came into effect on 10 September 2011.

The reliance on secondary legislation meant that other innovative aspects of the Equality Act could easily be shelved. Shortly after taking office, the Coalition government announced that it would not introduce the secondary legislation required to take forward the provisions for a socio-economic duty, a combined discrimination provision or for mandatory equal pay audits, meaning that much of the innovation in the Equality Act has been shelved. In addition, after a long delay in their formulation, the specific duties for the equality duty in England are more limited than those for its predecessor duties, having no direct provisions for equal pay or requirements to consult trade unions. The new specific duties covering England are far less prescriptive than those contained in the previous separate equality duties. Crucially, the recommendation to conduct EIAs is weaker as are the requirements to collect equality data and the requirement to consult stakeholders (see Hepple, 2011 and Fredman, 2011 for a detailed analysis). The Welsh Assembly and the Scottish Parliament have introduced more detailed and far reaching specific duties and it will be important to monitor how far this makes a difference to the application of the legislation.

The difficult passage of the Equality Act 2010 and the new Public Sector Equality Duty (PSED) demonstrates that seeking equality in public service delivery continues to be a politically charged and contested project. Neo-liberal political rhetoric has intensified since the 2010 general election, re-invoking fiscal austerity based on draconian measures to reduce eligibility for welfare and to provide a rationale for minimising state provision of public services. Legal challenges were successfully launched against cuts to public spending by government and local authorities, on the basis of disproportionate impact on the groups protected by the Duties (Conley, 2012a).[12] It is in this context that the Home Secretary and Equalities Minister, Teresa May announced on 1 May 2012, when the Specific Duties were barely a year old, that a review of the PSED would be conducted as part of the 'Red Tape Challenge', a government initiative to strip away bureaucratic burdens to business.

A range of outcomes of the review were possible with, ultimately, the threat that the Duty could be removed from the statute books completely. The consultation process was unorthodox in that it was not initially open to all stakeholders and was largely the remit of a government selected steering group. The role of the steering group was to define the methods of collecting evidence and to seek submissions of evidence on an invitation only basis. The response of stakeholder groups to the threat that loomed over the Public Sector Equality Duty was vocal and concerted. The problematic nature of the review process came under widespread public scrutiny and criticism when Doreen Lawrence OBE,[13] the mother of Stephen Lawrence, wrote an open letter to the Prime Minister, Deputy Prime Minister and other political leaders questioning the composition of the steering committee and highlighting its bias towards public service providers rather than public service users. The letter asked that the review should 'recognise that those who are to be held to account by legislation may have radically different views when compared to those who wish to use the legislation to hold public bodies to account'. As a result of strong support for these representations the review has been postponed.

The review of the Public Sector Equality Duty took place in an increasingly volatile context for equality and diversity. This volatility is likely to continue, as austerity measures introduced by the coalition government in response to the economic crisis have been and continue to be widely criticised for their disproportionate impact on already disadvantaged groups (MacLeavy, 2011; Williams-Findlay, 2011; Conley 2012b; Ginn, 2013; Rubery and Rafferty, 2013; Cross, 2013). There has been a resurgence of feminist activism, using the GED to challenge cuts in public services. National feminist campaigns such as the Fawcett Society and the Women's Budget Group are working alongside local campaigns to challenge the basis of budget cuts to local services and highlighting their disproportionate effect on women.[14]

Transnational protocols continue to be used nationally and locally to provide leverage for holding local authorities and the government to account. In 2013, the UK government report to CEDAW was challenged when delegates took up the issues identified in the shadow report, submitted by the Commission for Equality and Human Rights.[15] Concerns raised by the Committee included protection from discrimination under the Public Sector Equality Duty, the impact of austerity measures on women and women's services, and restrictions on women's access to legal aid.[16] While there are no UN sanctions to hold the UK government to account, the opportunities for transnational alliances formed at the convention offer potential leverage at local and national level.

Conclusion

In this chapter we have sought to provide an historical account of how feminist activists in Great Britain have worked in and against the state, in this instance the local state, to achieve public services that benefit women. It is important to note that a concern to bring women normally excluded from local democracy into democratic processes and to assert the social and economic value of care and of women's domestic work has underpinned feminist activism since the

1980s. Successive state administrations have resisted challenges to traditional gender roles within the family and attempts to address the politics of difference. In the face of political adversity from Conservative governments and rather lukewarm and unreliable support from Labour governments feminists have kept alive dreams and visions of the long agenda for women's equality by 'working the spaces of power' (Newman, 2012) within the changing landscape of women's equality work in government (Bashevkin, 2007; Eisenstein, 1991). This has often meant forging local and transnational feminist links when government support is absent, mobilising the coercive powers of supra national bodies to protect and advance a feminist agenda. When the political landscape at home is more receptive, feminist activists have lobbied for formal legislative measures that can hold public authorities, including the government, to account. Both strategies allow equality activists to create spaces within which transformative impacts are developed from policy discourse. Although sometimes limited to liberal short term measures, new strategy has sometimes prefigured larger social or governmental shifts (Cockburn, 1989; Newman, 2012). This work is precarious yet, as we will show in Chapters 4 and 5, has achieved significant results that are often rendered invisible within accounts that counterpose liberal and transformative impacts.

Our analysis, whilst specific to local government in Great Britain, parallels the analysis of femocracy in international contexts discussed in Chapter 2. In both contexts political ideology, strategy and stated organisational objectives did not and could not map directly onto each other, but were constructs shaped by the art of the possible at specific historical conjunctures. This necessary compromise might be read as an illustration of self-interested 'femocrats' selling out the feminist transformational agenda (Gelb, 1989; Eisenstein, 1991; Lovenduski and Randall, 1993). Alternatively it could be read as increased sophistication, as practitioners learned to hold their individual politics and purpose in tension with political agendas and organisational constraints (Meyerson and Scully, 1995; Kirton *et al.*, 2007). We turn in Chapters 4 and 5 to the voices of equality practitioners as they reflect on their lived experience of doing women's and gender equality work, attempting to harness the coercive power of the state for the benefit of women, over this period.

Notes

1 Criminal Justice and Public Order Act 1994.
2 The Greater London Council (GLC), led by Ken Livingstone, was a focal point for leading this opposition to the government, through a programme of extended local democracy (Coote and Campbell, 1982; Livingstone, 2011).
3 NAWO (www.nawo.org.uk/) provides some secretariat support and leadership for an alliance of about 100 NGOs, INGOs and other civil society groups – mainly women's and development organisations. The alliance is based on mutual interest in the annual UN Commission on the Status of Women (CSW). NAWO holds open meetings and has a Core group to liaise directly with government and two elected co-chairs. They set up working groups to produce issues and lobbying papers both for policy work directed outwards and for internal development. NAWO is recognised by government as the main civil society body with which to communicate on CSW.

4 The Women's National Commission (WNC), abolished by the Conservative government in 2010, was a government founded and sponsored organization established by a Labour government in 1969. It had two co-chairs, one government appointed and one elected by the Commission itself. The WNC's mission was 'to ensure by all possible means that the informed opinion of women is given due weight in government' (WNC, 1982). The commission had a requisite size of 50 organisations, which had to be national bodies with a large and active membership, including women's sections of unions and political parties (Gelb, 1989). Smaller feminist organisations were excluded, and the WNC policy reflected its membership that covered a broad political spectrum, of established women's organisations.

5 The Equality Standard for Local Government in England was established in 2001 through a partnership between the Commission for Racial Equality, the Disability Rights Commission, the Equal Opportunities Commission and the DIALOG unit of the Employers' Organisation for local government, with advice from the Audit Commission. It was linked to government resource allocation, and was replaced by the Local Government Equality Framework, 2009, which was not linked to resource allocation.

6 The IDeA was formed in 1998 as the Improvement and Development Agency for local government to work in partnership with all councils in England and Wales, to serve people and places better, to enhance the performance of the best local government authorities, accelerate the speed of improvement of the rest, and develop the sector as a whole. It was renamed the Local Government Improvement and Development Agency, its current title, in July 2010.

7 Earlier attempts to repeal the section 28 in 2000 were defeated in the House of Lords.

8 Stephen Lawrence was murdered in a racially motivated attack in 1993. His murderers were sentenced 19 years later in January 2012.

9 See Hansard http://www.publications.parliament.uk/pa/cm199900/cmhansrd/vo991130/text/91130w24.htm (accessed 23/6/2014).

10 See http://www.edf.org.uk/blog/?p=3 (accessed 23/6/2014).

11 Equality Act 2010 s.1.

12 See the Equality and Diversity Forum website, http://www.edf.org.uk/blog/?p=17719 for a useful list of the leading cases.

13 Doreen Lawrence was made a life peer in 2013, and is now Baroness Lawrence of Clarendon. She received an OBE in 2003 for services to community relations.

14 See for example www.fawcett.org.uk; www.wbg.org.uk.

15 See http://www.equalityhumanrights.com/human-rights/our-human-rights-work/international-framework/un-convention-on-the-elimination-of-discrimination-against-women/implementing-cedaw-in-britain/ (accessed 23/6/2014).

16 See http://www.edf.org.uk/blog/?p=28176 (accessed 23/6/2014).

4 Translating dreams into practice
Practitioner reflections

In this chapter we turn to the reflexive accounts of feminist equalities practitioners of their experiences of doing women's equality work in Labour administrations during the period covered by the research reviewed in Chapter 3. The research presented in this chapter offers context and contrast to the accounts of equality practitioners that follow, relating to the later period when the Gender Equality Duty was in place (Chapter 5). It was prompted by the contrast between these accounts and our own remembered experiences of feminist equality practice in the 1980s and 1990s. In our analysis of these contrasting narratives, we intended to investigate how feminist equality practitioners engaged with the workings of institutional power in a changing political context.

Feminist research into the practice of doing women's and gender equality work in local government has, as we have shown in Chapter 3, mainly been preoccupied with the potential and limitations of its strategies and outcomes. Research discussed in Chapter 2 highlighted the inevitable tensions between feminist movement aspirations and the politics of political parties in power. Similarly, research on femocracy and equality practice in Chapter 3 referred to political and organisational constraints, compromise and conflicting loyalties and accountabilities (Eisenstein, 1996; Lovenduski and Randall, 1993). The tone of much of this feminist research has been negative because of disappointment at limited outcomes and failure to deliver transformational, systemic change. The accounts that follow signpost what it was like to live out the contested and conflictual qualities of doing gender equality work, the passion and resilience required to sustain it, and how this both supported and placed its own limitations on what was essentially a collaborative political project.

To investigate this territory, Margaret, who had been a woman's equality advisor in a London local authority in the 1980s, invited seven feminist gender equality practitioners to join her in reflecting on their experiences of doing equality work in the 1980s and 1990s, and the vision and purpose that had inspired them at that time. The research was conducted through a series of reflective conversations, to which the researcher brought her experience as a feminist equality practitioner (Maynard and Purvis, 1994; Stanley, 1990). The purpose was to engage participants in a retrospective reflexive co-inquiry, reflecting on what their experiences of doing women's equality work in local government in Left Labour authorities had been like at the time, what values and vision had inspired and informed their strategies and practices, and how these might now have changed.

Six individual conversations and one small group discussion took place with women who had worked in a variety of different roles to promote women's equality in Labour local authorities in the 1980s and early 1990s. The conversations were framed as a participative inquiry (Maguire, 2001) into how each participant perceived her sense of purpose in the context in which she had then been working towards women's equality in local government, what had been achieved, and what she now thought could usefully be learned that might inform gender equality practice in the current context. The inquiry was grounded in a temporal and political context, of Left Labour administrations in local authorities, that was held in common, and which we each recognised. The process of co-inquiry that developed within each conversation had qualities similar to collective biography, where individual accounts of remembered experience associated with an event or an activity in the present are shared and 'witnessed', as a lens for critical inquiry into how to make sense of a present context (Haug *et al.*, 1987; Davies and Gannon, 2006). Video recordings of the conversations captured their emotional tone and quality and throughout the recordings there was a sense of enjoyment and of mutual recognition, affirming through the research an experience of having played a part in making history and, in its recording, asserting the value and meaning of the work. Alongside this was sadness at loss of political vision and of context in which women's equality was embedded in local democracy, and in which there was feminist activism in relation to the local state. It was as if the conversations provided an opportunity to witness and to record significant experiences that had been lost from public view and memory. The inquiry process that developed enabled us to reflect within the conversations on the purpose and meanings we had brought to our equality work during this period, how this had informed the strategies developed, and what we now considered to be its transformational potential.

The research participants

The research participants were identified through local professional and feminist networks. They are representative of a broadly shared feminist and socialist political stance but are not intended to be representative either in terms of feminist stance or in terms of ethnicity, age, sexuality or disability. Each had played a key role in developing the first phases of local authority women's equality work discussed Chapter 3. Clara had been a political leader, Sylvia and Laura had been heads of women's units, Hilary a women's equality advisor, Anna a community services liaison officer, Emma a community representative on a women's committee, and Gillian an independent activist and leading member of a feminist campaigning organisation. Three of them spoke of their experiences of being women's equality advisors, at different levels of seniority, in seven different London local authority women's units, including the GLC and GLA. One participant spoke of being part of a group of Left Labour Party members and trade unionists who set up a women's committee in the early 1980s, inspired by London, but in a different city. Two others spoke of their work with local authorities as feminist activists, one as an independent advisor representing older women on a women's committee, another as a service directorate equality advisor, and the other as a member of a national feminist campaigning organisation, who played a leading role in organising feminist participation in UN conferences on women in Nairobi in 1990 and Beijing in 1995. While they had come into these roles by a variety of different professional routes (education, legal advice, community development), only two had a prior history of local authority work, and all except two had socialist and/or feminist activist experience and backgrounds. Each of the participants continued to develop their equalities practice in other organisational contexts. Four of them, like Margaret, had continued to develop this work as self-employed gender equality consultants into the 2000s, working nationally and in some cases internationally, and one served for 10 years as deputy leader before becoming the first woman political leader of her unitary district council. Their age profile, ranging from 50–93 years, reflects the period of time covered. Their trajectories, and changing roles briefly introduced in the biographies below, reflect the changing shape and forms of intervention created by socialist feminists active in and around local government during the period leading up to the Equalities Act 2010 (Chapter 3).

Box 4.1: Participant biographies[1]

Clara

In the 1970s and 1980s Clara was active in local politics, helping to unionise voluntary and community organisations and setting up a law centre to advise on employment rights. With others involved in left politics she helped to form a group within the Labour Party. Once elected they decided to set up 'something for women', modelled on the women's committees and units that were forming in London local authorities. Twenty years later, when she was elected as political leader of the local authority, she organised the first ever city-wide consultation of women in local communities as part of a major culture shift from inward to outward facing local democracy. She continues this work now as a local activist, and works as an equality consultant internationally and nationally, advising governments on implementing UN and Council of Europe conventions and protocols on gender equality, human rights and local democracy.

Sylvia

Sylvia was a socialist activist in the 1960s and 1970s. In 1983 she left a full time funded PhD at LSE to work for the GLC Women's Support Unit, soon after it was first set up. At the GLC she oversaw the conversion of a building to house a London-wide women's centre. Later she was responsible for equalities monitoring of expenditure, targets and objectives across all GLC services. She went on to be Head of a well-resourced Women's Unit in a London borough, under a newly elected Left Labour administration, until it was dismantled by an incoming Conservative administration in 1989. Following this she joined a team of independent local authority equality consultants, who helped develop and implement the national equality benchmarking tools – the Equality Standard and later the Equality Framework for Local Government. For 20 years she provided expert advice and training to local authorities on compliance with equalities legislation. She is now semi-retired, continuing to be a feminist activist and radical historian.

Anna

In the late 1970s and early 1980s Anna was part of a local network of feminist activists experimenting with collective childcare, new ways of living out sexual and gender relations, and disability and anti-racist politics. As a member of this network she helped to set up an independent community based Children's Centre, still in existence and a model for Children's Centres later set up under New Labour, most of which were closed under later austerity measures. She joined a London local authority to be a community services liaison officer during 1983–90. She then worked as a legal advisor for a national charity, where she continued to offer specialist advice on equality issues, until she retired.

Gillian

Gillian is a founder member of the National Alliance of Women's Organisations (NAWO[1]), a Trustee of the Friends of the Women's Library and former Board member of the Fawcett Society. She is an activist who helped to organise the NGO delegations to the UN conferences on women in Nairobi in 1985 and Beijing in 1995. She worked for many years in the 1990s and 2000s as an independent women's voluntary sector consultant and researcher, enabling feminist organisations to restructure and to expand their membership in the context of shrinking availability of local authority and charitable funding and the need to develop a business case for their services. She is now a writer, researcher and activist and continues to support many feminist organisations in a voluntary capacity.

Emma

In the mid-1980s Emma was one of eight advisory members representing different constituencies of women on the Women's Committee of an inner

London local authority, retiring in 1987. At this time she worked for a pensioners' organisation and was a self-employed training consultant for women, writer and poet. She has been an active feminist and member of lesbian, Jewish and older women's campaigns. In her 91st year, she is a member of an older women's group, a member of philosophy and creative writing classes, and continues to introduce feminist politics to members of the University of the Third Age.

Hilary

Prior to working in a London Women's Unit, Hilary was a teacher, doing gender equality policy work in education and involved in 1970s and 80s feminist networks. In 1991 she joined an inner London local authority Women's Unit and job shared as Head of Unit for a short while. In 1996 she went on to be the first Equal Opportunities officer in an outer London borough under a newly elected Labour administration, where she developed and put in place the first equal opportunities policies and systems in council departments. In 2001 she joined the Greater London Authority under Ken Livingston's Left Labour administration where she worked in the Department of Finance and Performance. One aspect of her work was to monitor performance and expenditure against equality targets in all GLA member organisations. She now works for a national charity.

Laura

Laura worked in teaching and social and care services in the voluntary and statutory sectors before becoming the head of a local authority Women's Unit in 1988. A feminist since the early 1970s, she developed and sustained the unit for nearly a decade, working closely with the core mission and delivery of the council, but bringing a radical gender perspective. Since then she has worked as a consultant in public and voluntary sectors on a wide spectrum of projects and programmes (especially public sector) many relating to women and equality, including women's employment and education in science, engineering and technology.

The conversations

Each conversation began with a question and an invitation: 'How would you describe now what you were setting out to achieve in the equality project you were engaged in then?' The purpose of the research was introduced with a reference to the accounts of practitioners in the later period, and to their contrast with the feminist political rationale for equality work that was part of my remembered experience. In the four sections that follow, the multifaceted narratives that emerged are organised into themes that explore the values and passions that had informed the work, the lived experience of exhilaration, danger and risk, the friendships and collective vision that sustained the work and the dilemmas encountered while inhabiting a contested and highly charged landscape of change. In the conclusions I identify cross cutting themes and reflect on the narratives that emerged.

'In and against the state': redistributing power and resources

> An image is coming into my head: Cockburn's 'in and against the state'. [Using the mechanisms of the local state – working to empower women outside the structures of the local state – using the resources of the local state to reach out to people]. It was all about opening out local government and bringing people in – reaching out and giving out resources.
>
> GLC, 1980s (Sylvia)

A consistent picture emerged from each of the conversations of coming together to transform local government from an inward looking, self-serving elite to an outward facing representative body in which women and other minorities were equally represented and resourced.

> We needed to change the way the organisation worked – there was a real sense of the council being quite excluding – a real sense of them and us. But it was also more about having a political presence, women being heard that was important not just making things better in terms of services but women being there at the table.
>
> (Clara)

In some conversations the focus was on equitable distribution and access to services as of right to local citizens, and to employees. From this perspective the work of promoting women's equality was about establishing rights upheld by rules that could then be invoked and challenged if not met.

> Citizens have a right to the services they need.
>
> (Anna)

In other parts of the conversations, participants described their work more in terms of providing opportunities to participate in public life that were right for women, and learning from feminist organisations about what women could bring to democratic process from a feminist, self-defined perspective. Speaking of the vision that had informed their work at this time, they emphasised that it was not simply about extending existing resources and services to make them available to more women, but more importantly about developing services that challenged the gendered division of labour, male violence and supported women's autonomy:

> We were challenging the idea of a deficit model. Yes, women should have more of what men got, but we also focused on what different services, as in

new, and what better services, as in woman-centred services, they should get. I still think that more, better, different is a way to think about services and the role of the state in relation to women.

(Laura)

Radical challenge to established practice was made both by internal redistribution of resources through politically driven controls, and by extending democracy outwards, so that women took part in democratic decision making. Each participant spoke of the use of hierarchical power as a necessary strategy for achieving fair distribution of resources, through regimes of compliance driven by top down coercive change. Three of the participants spoke of how important their experience of working in The Greater London Council (GLC)[2] Women's' Unit, and later the Greater London Authority (GLA),[3] had been as an incubator for these strategies, structures and processes for promoting equality, which they then took into other local authorities. Within the GLC and its successor body, the GLA, equality work was given high profile support by the political leadership. Large budgets and operational authority for managers and equalities support staff meant that the GLC and the GLA became sites where strategy and practice were developed for redistributing resources towards equality groups, and extending democratic representation outwards. Within these London-wide bodies, the political leadership drew upon substantial legal powers to require compliance with strategic initiatives to redistribute resources through budgetary controls.

Hilary described how, when she joined the GLA in 2001, redistribution of resources was effectively achieved through a robust system of equality targets and monitoring in the finance office, linked to performance management. Leadership by individuals committed to the political project was, she stated, 'the engine that made rules work'.

> [In the GLA] we drilled right down to how budgets were spent, setting targets following through and monitoring and publishing results – using pie charts and number crunching. This did effect change – people got the message that if you want to get on you have to demonstrate you have got your percentage of women in senior management! It worked!
>
> (Hilary)

She contrasted this strategy, where equalities work was located in finance and run by senior men appointed with a brief to use top down power to enforce compliance, with the Women's Committee and Unit in her local authority who were less senior and who relied on influence achieved through relationships built with senior managers and politicians. Activities to extend democracy outwards by creating mechanisms for direct representation and consultation were a dramatic challenge and shock to the culture of an inward facing overwhelmingly male and white establishment civil service (Livingstone, 2011; Webb, 2001).

Alongside this narrative of legitimate use of top down coercive power to effect redistribution of resources was a different narrative, of a more emergent process of change within an extended local democracy, rooted in local networks in which change was inspired by collective acts of imagination. Change here was to be bottom up, translated from social movements into the state bureaucracy by local authority equality advisors and politicians. Linked to this was a narrative of accountability to local citizens, and rights for women to take up their fair share of resources in their role as local citizens, taxpayers and voters. In Anna's and Clara's case, for example, the mechanism for change was not legal compliance but political leadership embedded in local activist networks in which council staff, politicians and trade unionists were all key players. Anna's manager came from a Left Labour Party background, as did the political leader of the local authority, and both were participants in activist networks in local communities. Her manager asked her to develop processes in which local authority staff and local citizens within equality groups jointly identified priorities, and allocated resources for service development:

> What was innovative were the cross directorate working groups, made up of women employees, at all levels, from manual workers to senior managers, and women from local communities. The groups brought together women employees, with members of local communities, and women managers with manual workers, to address employment and service issues. There was assertiveness training for women, to enable them to take part. The lesbian group organised the first ever borough-wide festival, at which each service directorate had to display information about their services and policy. Women employees could do their paid work in these groups. Libraries were required to have books for lesbians and disabled groups freely available and accessible. The disability group employed their own builder and architect to enable access to parks, for example, signposting in Braille, picnic tables, ramps – all of which are still in place.
>
> London local authority, 1980s (Anna)

This clearly articulated vision of women in diverse local communities actively participating in an extended local democracy, emerged in conversation with participants speaking of the first phases of women's equality work, the period described in Chapter 3 as 'municipal feminism' (Bruegel and Kean, 1995). Each spoke from their practice and experience of being a community activist, political leader or equality advisor, of the mechanisms for more equitable redistribution of resources for council services and employment, but beyond this for direct access to power and governance for women.

Power, courage and risk

> At the end of the day it's about power and how individuals use power.
>
> (Hilary)

> Not on the streets nor in the community, but inside local government
> I developed my understanding of power and the highly political nature of
> women's equality work!
>
> (Laura)

In the early phases of equality work, politicians and their staff experienced
vulnerability to sustained sexist ridicule, and opposition from the media and
central government. Under this pressure political divisions often opened up
within the Labour Party and being associated with leadership on equality issues
was seen by some as a career risk and sacrifice for staff and politicians.

> It's a brave thing to do, but you do experience discrimination.
>
> (Hilary)

In local authorities where Labour administrations were defeated, equality
policy was often the first to be abolished. The depth of hostility directed at
the equality project and what it came to represent was shown in the violence
with which some of the units were dismantled. In one local authority, all the
equality units were closed and files that could be used to discredit the work
were locked away by the incoming administration the day after they were
elected.

> The Tories came in the day after the [local] election in 1990 and they got
> officer hench people and took the filing cabinets in the race unit and threw
> them on their faces, and locked them in another room. They closed down
> the unit, and made us redundant.
>
> (Sylvia)

In this embattled context, the political priorities and affiliation of the Women's
Committee Chair were important determinants of the scope of the work that
women's equality advisors were able to undertake. Equality advisors had to
reconcile party political agendas with their own values and assessment of priority.
Decisions could be difficult and contentious, for example, where feminist political
differences were played out within women's units and in their relations with
external campaigns.

Sylvia described how she arrived at a tactical compromise to resolve a conflict
between the Women's Unit work with lesbian communities and a request from
her Chief Executive to censor lesbian films in order to comply with legislation
that outlawed promotion of lesbian and gay rights. She refused to comply with the
requirement to censor the films, but did this in a tactical way by agreeing to say
that the films did not consciously 'promote homosexuality'.

> It was International Women's Week and we [the Women's Unit] had films
> on at the local cinema. The Chief Executive called me in and asked me to
> go and view all the lesbian films showing and to say that they did not

contravene Section 28 [of the Local Government Act, see Section 1 of this chapter]. I refused because I thought that was giving in to Section 28. I said 'I'm not doing it and if you have to discipline me so be it.' She worked out a form of words I could write, something to say that they don't consciously promote homosexuality, and I decided tactically it would be the right thing to do. I felt uncomfortable saying that as it was kind of colluding with Section 28, but on the other hand it meant that the films could still be shown.

(Sylvia)

Conflict between political principle and pressure to compromise was strongest when there were close links with vibrant feminist and anti-racist movements, and faded with the decline of independent organisation. These close links introduced tensions where they came into conflict with the political priorities of the Chair of the Women's Committee or her political party. Work with lesbian communities was often a touchstone for divisions within the Labour Party.

In my local authority, the left/right battle within the Labour group was fought out over control of the Women's Committee. When the left wing chair of the committee was deposed by the right wing, the new Chair had a different and essentially liberal agenda, did not want us to work with lesbians, and preferred us to focus on older women and carers.

(Sylvia)

Lead politicians and equality advisors had to manage the tension between feminist agendas of their own and of their constituents whilst navigating party and management accountabilities. Women's equality committees were vulnerable to internal conflict, for instance between new and old left within the Labour Party. Women's equality advisors and committee members were often perceived to be new arrivals, whose influence was determined by the fortunes of their political sponsors. As such, their relationship with lead politicians was crucial and a change of political leadership or Chair could mean a change of direction between radical or more conservative priorities. As we have seen from the feminist literature on femocrats working with changing political regimes in Australia (Chapter 2), while some saw compromise as betrayal of ideals, others took the view that it was necessary to 'cut your cloth' to what was possible in the local government context (Eisenstein, 1996).

The first women's equality advisors were often recruited on the basis of their feminist politics (Cockburn, 1989). Our conversations explored the dilemmas and challenge that this posed for how to apply feminist principles within the bureaucratic structures and political accountabilities of local government. Experience of how to operationalise equality within the complex politics and bureaucratic structures of local government was not, on the whole, what advisors brought with them. Strategic skill to make change happen had to be developed in and through practice. Expectations were often unrealistic and this brought its own challenges.

> It all felt very exciting that we had women in the council we could relate to ... this was a means of collecting views and issues and then getting something done internally.
>
> (Clara)

Getting something done about issues women identified was not a smooth process, and in some cases fairly rapidly became confrontational, for example, in relation to equal pay and job evaluation. There was 'respect for what was done and frustration'.

> Frequently council reports commented that there were no implications for women. We would ask, if 50 per cent of the population were not affected why would we be spending money on it?"
>
> (Clara)

Stress related to the breadth of the project and difficulty in managing expectations in the Women's Unit sometimes led to long term staff sickness.

> They were trying to do impossible jobs. The weight of expectation, trying to keep the women's unit as open as possible to a lot of casework and respond to internal pressures to provide a gender impact analysis on service plans and decisions for the entire council was ridiculous.
>
> (Clara)

Participants spoke of how mechanisms for converting knowledge into actionable plans within the local government bureaucracy were invented and developed over time. Compliance with policy developed by women's equality advisors through departmental accountability to the women's and equality committees was the key mechanism in the first decades of equality work. Capacity to make change happen was reliant on equality advisors' successfully establishing internal credibility within political and management leadership and on their willingness to use their authority to translate plans into practice.

> I remember when I first started, I suppose naively, being frustrated by this call for research and data to justify our policy proposals. Didn't we know what needed to be done, what needed to change? Years of feminist analysis had showed us. But we obliged and sought diligently for facts and figures. And they were often quite difficult to get – with a lack of appropriate research and disaggregated data. This was what we would now call evidence. Evidence based policy! Ironically after all the effort, we often found that these facts, and statements of need from consultations, didn't necessarily, automatically result in policy or practice changes. The climate was still one in which

many officers and politicians seem to deny the need for any more 'equality' for women. So, facts are not enough, the voices of women are not enough.

(Laura)

In our conversations a picture emerged of the embattled and highly charged emotional territory of equality work as it was first being established in local government. Working to the long agenda, women's equality in the context of extended local democracy, was ground breaking and exciting for the feminists and socialists leading the project, but was perceived by some as a career risk. The use of top down coercive political power to effect change challenged established hierarchies within local authorities but also evoked considerable hostility, and even ridicule. The bottom up extended democratic processes were attacked by Conservative local government. Both strategies required leadership and sponsorship from powerful political leaders and senior managers. The compromises that had to be made often evoked challenge from and conflict with feminist constituents, and this external conflict put pressure on collaborative relationships that had to be managed internally.

Working with the politics of difference

There was this rather inelegant phrase we used for quite a while: women are not a homogeneous group, and then a list of different kinds of women, which grew and shrank with fashions in equalities work and local government. But it meant something worthwhile – we were committed to working on the interests of different, diverse groups of women. Our approach was to address these interests through targeted projects or by integrating their various and potential perspectives into generic policy or service developments for women. I think this was pioneering. It is still being struggled with through ideas of diversity, intersectionality and inclusivity for example, and a precursor of a customer orientation. Our work often fell short of the powerful aspirations for inclusivity we and others had, but we made up for this through our intense awareness of the challenge and keeping the intention on the agenda.

(Laura)

Working with the politics of difference emerged as a core dimension of the work of Women's Units. As we have seen in Chapter 2, in the early days of gender equality work, understanding the need to address diversity between women grew from connections established between women's organisations and communities, and from the close working relationships established between colleagues. These relationships, while sometimes conflicted, did establish a context for learning about and engaging with the complexity of women's lived experience. However this was not straightforward, as feelings of betrayal sometimes accompanied political compromise. Women's committees and equality practitioners had to steer a difficult path where there were political conflicts between groups or where women's initiative challenged established male dominance within minority communities, for example, in relation to Southall Black Sisters' work on domestic violence:[4]

> They [Southall Black Sisters] were challenging male dominance within the Asian community and domestic violence, but I knew they were incredibly important for women experiencing domestic violence and I continued to argue for them and make sure the bureaucracy did not subvert them and that they continued to get their grant.
>
> (Sylvia)

In conversation, participants' stories referred to how they had addressed diversity of priority and need in a variety of ways, including grant aid targeted towards specific ethnic minority community based projects, direct representation on political committees of advisors from a variety of ethnic communities and specified equality categories, consultation and research as a basis for service design and development, training and employment.

> We organised the first ever international conference for refugee women.
>
> (Sylvia)

This meant challenging, head on, established beliefs embedded in the discourse of welfare (see Chapters 2 and 3) about women's place in the family and inviting women to define their capacities and needs on their own terms whether disabled, black and minority ethnic, older or younger women and/or lesbians.

> I am proud of the way we introduced new, controversial or neglected subjects onto the political and policy agendas of the local state, encouraged by women and feminists inside and outside the Labour Party. Many of these issues are still unresolved challenges to equality today, being revisited by new champions, new political forms, and through new media. Alternatively they have – to an extent – become subjects for the mainstream and a recognised part of the wider political agenda. They include racial equality, child care, sexual and domestic violence, FGM, gay and lesbian rights. As well as the new subjects, we introduced new methods, innovating with community involvement, multi-agency interventions and strategies on domestic violence, outcome orientated women's action plans, gender and race audits and gender performance indicators.
>
> (Laura)

Transformation of service delivery, a stated objective, was the aim and result of work with self-organised external groups, and internally with senior managers in service departments. Housing, education, leisure, refuse collection and more, all were challenged to change service delivery patterns in order to take into account a range of specific needs of women in diverse communities, and to work alongside independent organisations. Alongside this, forums for women employees addressed issues such as sexual, homophobic and racial harassment, equal pay, disabled access, flexible working hours, and access to training, recruitment and promotion. Committee reports which participants had written and to which they referred spoke of myriad local self-organised projects such as women's refuges, reproductive health, support for women with disabilities, carers, childcare, translation and interpretation services for specific communities, girls projects, older women's projects, and many specific needs within minority ethnic communities were named, addressed and resourced. An important dimension of this work was to affirm and celebrate women's self-organisation and achievements in ways that explored and affirmed new ways of being women, in relation to children, to men and each other, living challenge to established gender relations, effectively 'doing gender differently' (Scott, 2002).

> The three powerful strong women who were appointed established the Women's Unit as a physical presence in the town hall, going out and talking to women in local communities as well as taking up cases of discrimination, not just for women employed in the local authority, but for health and other services.
>
> (Clara)

Many of the women's equality units held budgets to fund and publicise events in International Women's Week; typically these were cultural, poetry, music, dance and cabaret organised by feminist campaigns and networks within minority ethnic and local communities. They brought together artists, performers and campaigners within local communities, subverting gender norms and affirming women's creativity and resilience through music, dance, art, theatre, humour, developing different ways of thinking and of representing women's lives. In conversation it was felt that these processes of coming together to campaign and to celebrate touched and transformed many women's lives in ways that could not be quantified or easily measured. This cultural work helped to build a sense of entitlement for women in diverse communities to equal access to decision making such as advisory membership of women's committees. Funding, publicising and supporting the activities were important dimensions of the work of equality units.

The separate organisation of resources for equality groups, through different committees and units, itself an attempt to ensure equal access, inevitably led to competition for influence and resources within political processes and structures. There was sometimes a loss of fluidity in how differences between women were addressed and voiced, as competition developed for limited equalities budgets. Participants emphasised that within and between equality units there was commitment to synthesis, and to avoiding destructive debates on the hierarchy of oppression, and stressed solidarity established with women across equality strands, despite political conflicts within and between local communities. The challenge of how to translate intersections of discrimination and disadvantage into organisational practice remains, and is all the more pressing as generic have replaced single equality duties and equality advisors, and this we consider in greater detail in Chapter 5.

Structure and change agency: compliance and political leadership

> If you are in a position of power you can get things done!
>
> GLA (Hilary)

> Leaders are very important but you have to have a structure that allows them to be.
>
> Feminist organisation (Gillian)

A strong theme that emerged from each of our conversations was access to political power and leadership to effect change within the local state. Central to this theme was the key role played by political leaders and champions within local authorities, including both male and female managers and politicians who set up the political and operational structures and processes to translate political vision into practice. Participants spoke of systems that they had created to support two ways of exercising power: top down coercive power to achieve compliance with prescriptive policy objectives, and mobilising the power of women in local communities through democratic processes to create a more emergent vision of equality and change.

> In our Labour Group we adopted a policy that at least 50 per cent of the elected positions had to be held by women. This included committee chairs as well as internal group positions such as whip. It meant that we got positions earlier than we might of otherwise and had the opportunity to show we were better than – or no worse than the men. The critical mass made a difference.
>
> (Clara)

While many of the stories relating to the early period referred to dependence on powerful political sponsors, participants also spoke of how in the later period they had accessed and exercised power themselves, either as independent consultants or as political leaders. To illustrate this we present two contrasting stories: Sylvia who became an equality consultant working with a national network of specialists in public services in the late 1990s and early 2000s, leading up to and including the period when the positive equality duties had first been introduced, and Clara who became a political leader for a brief period in 2002, and then an international gender mainstreaming consultant.

Sylvia's story: gender equality through enforcement and compliance

> I use the Gender Equality Duty to get my foot in the door and kick, to go in and say 'you are required to do x', then through the training make them

see 'in a softer way' the impact of discrimination and of difference, enabling them to make a perceptual shift through reflection with colleagues on their own experiences of discrimination.

Sylvia became a freelance equalities consultant after her job as head of a women's equality unit in a local authority came to an end with a change in political administration in 1991. Her story illustrates the power of working as an external change agent, commissioned by managers to use her expertise to expose discrimination and recommend measures for legal compliance.

In the early 1990s, Sylvia was commissioned to conduct equality audits by individual managers who she described as change agents. While at the time there was anti-discrimination legislation, there was no legal requirement to promote equality (Chapter 3). However the concept of audit allowed managers who cared about equality to call her in to 'just find out what's going on', to uncover hidden race, gender or disability discrimination. This work was led by individual managers with support from politicians, and was not by any means limited to Labour boroughs. Sometimes there was backlash, as in the case of the London Fire Brigade where what was exposed through her work was sexualised and sexist behaviour and culture.

In the late Thatcher years, however, equality 'simply dropped off the agenda' until the implementation of the Disability Discrimination Act in 1995, which brought renewed interest in equalities, and following the implementation of the RRA (2000) from 2002. The legal requirement to produce race equality schemes, the shift from 'thou shalt not' to 'thou shalt' introduced by the positive duty to promote equality was in her view 'a watershed and a sea change' (see Chapter 3). For example, it allowed a socialist feminist manager under a Conservative administration in a London borough to commission Sylvia to help produce one of the first Race Equality Schemes in a London borough.

In the late 1990s, under the Labour national administration, Sylvia had worked with a local government umbrella body to put together the Equality Standard, an equality benchmarking tool linked to resource allocation for local authorities and public services. Sylvia, along with equality consultants and trainers registered with this body, worked with local authorities to put equality schemes together and raise the quality of equality practice. Her observation was that while the Equality Standard mattered more to local authorities than the law, because it was linked to resource allocation, the quality of schemes produced was often poor, with little recognition of specificity between strands and a tendency to cut and paste across schemes.

> There was general bafflement at how to consult on gender, and reliance on women's organisations to consult with. Moreover, there was a loss of vision that people were gendered. Despite the requirement in the Equality Standard to comply with equality legislation, over and over again they disappeared gender.

Sylvia and her colleagues were able to address this more directly after the Gender Equality Duty came into effect in 2007. Central government money was made available, through the local government support agency, to provide free training to public bodies to comply with the positive equality duties and prepare for their assessment of performance on equality as measured by the Equality Standard.

Sylvia described her work to promote gender equality throughout this period as having two dimensions. On the one hand, managers and equality advisors 'brought me in as an enforcer' to enable organisations to comply with audit and, once legislation had been introduced, with the legal duties. On the other hand, once she had gained entry she worked in a 'softer way' to achieve a 'perceptual shift'. National equality benchmarking provided a framework for doing this 'softer' work, and this is a theme taken up by equality practitioners implementing the GED in the period that followed (Chapter 5).

Her story demonstrates how, in the period where political support for equality units had been withdrawn, former equality advisors were able to apply their experience in an external expert consultancy role to support internal equality advocates. In this role they were able to use their knowledge of internal systems and of legislation to support the long agenda for equality work:

> Not being rule bound – but using rules skilfully to maximise their impact and to promote equality – stretching the legal framework, like pizza dough.

During this period she noted a loss of gendered perspective. While gender equality could be introduced as a dimension of race or disability work, specific work to promote gender, until Gender Equality Duty was introduced in 2006, relied on the commitment of individual managers and politicians, who were prepared to 'stretch' the legal framework to achieve change.

Clara's story: gender equality through political leadership

> I believed it was important for me to model being a woman leader, in a way that would set a different tone. It was important to be in a position to make these things happen.

In 2002 Clara was elected leader of her local authority. Twenty years previously she had been one of a group of community activists and trade unionists who decided to join the Labour Party and stand for election.

When elected as leader, Clara realised she had just a year in office before elections would take place. She decided to make it a priority to promote women's equality. Arguing that equality was a responsibility of leadership, she modelled outward facing leadership and instituted mechanisms for individual employees at any level of seniority in the local authority and members of the public to come and talk to her about issues related to local authority service, and with the help of voluntary and community organisations organised a far reaching consultation exercise and conference with women in local communities.

We needed to change the way the organisation worked, it was very much them and us … this was about women being heard, and there at the table.

Her approach to promoting equality was to develop mechanisms for embedding equality as a strong dimension of local democracy, leading a culture shift within the council administration from being inward to outward facing in service delivery and governance:

> I tried to talk to as many groups and organisations as possible. I set up so that anybody who was a registered elector or a child going to school or university could make an appointment to come and see me or any member of staff could and I had loads of people coming to see me and I learned so much about what was going on in the city that you would not have found out otherwise and particularly in the council as an employer.

Clara's approach to equality work had, she stated, two 'arms': to set up mechanisms to integrate equality into mainstream processes for resource allocation, and to bring women to the table.

> One arm was to set up mechanisms such as an equalities action group to look at the equality implications of community strategy. And with other partners, we made the council budget align with the community strategy so one followed the other instead of being separate.
>
> Then the other arm was to say no one has consulted women in the city about what should be priorities or community strategy. So we funded outreach work, it's still the biggest consultation the council ever did. We worked with community organisations and funded the conference, with transport and child care and real time voting. We had identified in consultation key issues for the community strategy and then women at the conference voted on what they thought were priorities, and then managers had to find a way of addressing these in the community strategy … it was really powerful!

In contrast to the risks and costs of leading on equality in earlier periods that were described by Hilary, Clara spoke of widespread support she had encountered from council staff for this shift towards a more outward facing focus and local accountability.

> There was a massive appetite for people in the council wanting change … and people would kind of say 'we can't tell you how pleased we are'.

Clara's story illustrates the potential for feminist leadership to embed women's equality at the core of outward facing local democracy at a particular point in time when there was an appetite for change. In contrast to the earlier phase of equality work, when political leaders first instigated the shift towards outward facing local democracy, almost two decades later Clara had the political support to instigate these changes from a formal position of leadership. Her feminist political leadership was the driver for developing mechanisms to enable women to become active participants in local democracy and for embedding priorities they had identified within internal processes for resource allocation. Moreover her open door for hearing directly from individual employees and members of local communities supported an open democratic style of leading that signalled a shift of focus towards local constituents, went beyond formal mechanisms. Her story illustrates the potential that can be unleashed when women committed to equality enable participation through their leadership.

Changing the world: sustaining momentum

> We thought we'd change the world, and we probably thought bigger than most other organisations now. That sense of optimism, of anything being possible, is probably gone.
>
> (Gillian)

> I think there was a point when because it was high up on the agenda at least people had to nod in that direction, and now it's fallen off.
>
> (Clara)

Each conversation ended with reflections on what had been achieved then, and could be sustained now, in a context that had radically changed. While there was agreement that gender equality had 'fallen off the agenda' within public services, this was tempered by a view that legislation, and equality benchmarking linked to resourcing, had established an acceptance within local government that 'we have to do this':

> There is a willingness now that there wasn't in mid-90s – People kind of know they have to buy it. It's because of the law.
>
> (Sylvia)

> We have succeeded in getting these issues onto the agenda. The discourse is easier in all sorts of circles.
>
> (Hilary)

Alongside this was the view that without political drivers, legislation and business processes could not succeed. Clara spoke of deliberations with colleagues working with politicians on implementing the European Charter on Equality in emerging new democracies:

CLARA: You have to think, why would a politician say equality for women is important? If you had someone committed politically, how would they convince their colleagues, what support would you need to give them to support the arguments? And a lot of what we came up with was, this is 51 per cent of your vote … if you are not overtly acknowledging women's issues and concerns, why should they vote for you? And being able to show where people had taken account of women's issues they were not just popular for women but the rest of the population.

INTERVIEWER: Do you think it's possible to demonstrate that?

CLARA: If you bring it down to those crude levels quite a lot do get that … and by and large you can start with the assumption that most people elected to political office are motivated by the desire to do good, if you can tap into that joint thing it does help and it was a way to get people to argue that resource should go there.

INTERVIEWER: Quite often public opinion doesn't support …

CLARA: Where you have got to spend money on a perceived minority interest that's more difficult, where it comes down to a political decision. At the end of the day you are making a political judgement. There may not be a business case, so then you are thrown back on people's political motivation, or their political beliefs, and not everyone is going to agree … at the end of the day, you need somebody who is prepared to stand up for that and that's where it's been much more difficult, and I know there was a focus on minority issues and why are we spending money and that sort of thing but I think now, now the focus on almost everything the LA [local authority] does is perceived to be misspending our money even provision of very basic services means everything is under scrutiny, so it's very difficult for people to stand up and say we are doing this because it's the right thing to do.

Those who had been working as equality advisors felt that the whole scope of change that had been achieved was small scale, but this did not diminish the significance of the changes that had been achieved in women's lives as a result of the work.

It was carried out in a small window of opportunity when we were given a little money and 'allowed' to do the work. EOP is a squiggle compared to a thick black line that is the real stuff. The squiggle has made a massive difference to women's lives. It hasn't changed the overall balance of power between men and women and this has in many ways worsened. But this doesn't mean it was not worth doing or did not benefit many women.

(Hilary)

However, some of those employed in the early phases of equality work felt that change in the governance and organisation of public services had been so extensive that the skills and strategies developed were no longer applicable:

The nub of it is the changing role of LAs [Local Authorities]. It's partly the cuts – many local authorities can't provide services that they don't have to by law. But it's also the increasing privatisation of services – domiciliary care, free schools and so on. Things that the local authority used to do directly are now going out to tender to private companies ... I don't know how you work in that environment where LAs can't provide essential services and no longer have overall responsibility for what's really needed.

(Anna)

Modernisation of public services had brought opportunities in the organisation of equality as well as difficulties.

There was a huge feeling, not just about women, that local government exists for local government – actually the people out there are a bit of a nuisance rather than your whole reason for being and I think local government's got better about that but there's still not enough real thinking through of what that means.

(Clara)

In the face of adversity and the crumbling of democratic structures, new methods and ways of thinking about continuity and change were necessary. Achievements and strategies developed within a context that had now disappeared needed to be recorded and remembered because they affirmed a sense of possibility, within a wider vision. This was evidenced and symbolised in accounts by those who had taken part in transnational events, such as the NGO conferences that brought together women across contexts and communities, to develop common purpose and solidarity across different context and priorities. Speaking of the UN Fourth World Conference on Women, Beijing, 1995, Gillian affirmed how important the experience of coming together as women was as a source of inspiration and motivation:

I went to Beijing, which was extremely difficult and expensive and very uncomfortable, and yet it was the strongest emotional charge I had felt almost anywhere, to be with those women who had struggled from all over the world to get there. Undoubtedly, coming together as women was the most exciting thing about it. These were mega events.

(Gillian)

There was a sense of recognition and of friendship that came through in the interviews. It was as if the act of revisiting remembered experience as part of a research process with others who had been active in a shared moment of history affirmed a wider vision of a women's equality project that could not be contained within any specific context, but which needed to evolve and change. The sense of optimism of the early period had gone, but hope and desire for transformative change had regenerated in the present:

The Women's National Commission which was doing a lot of follow up work was just removed from the face of the world by this government. So I think that sense of optimism and everything being possible probably is no longer. But one thing I do think about is that while older feminist groups may have difficulty recruiting there are very strong groups of younger feminist women who are confident and are creating their own agendas.

(Gillian)

We have to inaugurate change of our own now – no one is going to do it for us! We have to decide what we want and what we want to change and get co-operation – that's the hardest part.

(Emma)

What came through in taking stock of the past in these conversations was a sense of creative imagination, sparked within the process of co-inquiry. It seemed important to hold and to share the memory of what had been achieved, not in order to replicate what was created in the past, but in order to retain a sense of possibility, a confidence that women can engage with a changing context to co-create a feminist future.

The conversations seemed to rekindle the passion and sense of possibility in coming together as feminists to work towards the common end of women's equality, in and through democratic processes that were also changing. As equalities advisors, political leaders and activists we had been at the interface between visions of what might be, and the reality of what could be. Compromise of principle in order to work within political and organisational constraints was sometimes experienced as betrayal of feminist political values and of each other, and these conflicts could be persecuting and difficult to manage. Stories were told of these betrayals and conflicts but also of the exhilaration of coming together as women working towards equality. We spoke of the emotional demands of sustaining working relationships in this environment and how it had often led to burnout. In contrast, the recordings demonstrate the powerful emotional impact of the experience of positive collaboration for change, and that this was held in memory, and continued to add yeast to our work in new contexts, within which new alliances could be sought and made.

Concluding reflections

In these conversations we reviewed the challenges and opportunities that were experienced as we pursued the long agenda for change during the 1980s, and how these were followed through and developed in the 1990s and early 2000s. As author, I do not claim that these accounts were complete, or impartial. Rather I suggest the narrative that emerged was specific to its temporal and political context, and to the perceptions and experiences of a set of actors, and who were white, diverse in age, sexuality, and ethnicity and shared a political lens that could broadly be called 'socialist feminist'. We drew from experiences that spanned three decades of equality work in local government and public services. While none of the participants continued to work in public services, and half were retired from employment, all continued to be actively engaged in feminist networks and subsequent to employment in public services had introduced their knowledge and experience of feminist change practice into other organisational contexts.

In authoring this chapter I recognise that memories are partial, and that there are many more stories to be told by key actors with radical, socialist and liberal feminist activist perspectives, each informed by experiences of race, gender, sexuality, class, disability and differently positioned in institutional, temporal and historical contexts. I nevertheless saw a value in surfacing aspects of the lived experiences of developing equality strategy and practice that have not been the focus of published research. This was not in the service of nostalgia or to read back into the past a narrative that belongs to the present (Hemmings, 2011), but in order to record and reach an understanding of the cost and risks, as well as the achievements, of feminist equality practice in the local state. The question of how feminists can sustain and develop the practice of promoting equality in specific temporal and political contexts, at the interface between feminist organising and institutional power, has no easy resolution. Feminist archive projects offer scope for investigating the experiences of different actors in the early phases of equality work, and how the dreams of equality that inspired them are taken up, discarded or displaced by newer generations of feminists (see, for example, the *Sisterhood and After* British Library project).[5] This chapter signposts scope for critical reflection on what may have been lost from memory when previous challenge and achievements are viewed through the lens of the present.

What was at stake, for us and indeed many practitioners of this time, was an opportunity for radical redistribution of resources towards women in marginalised groups, access to decision making within local democratic structures, and an attempt to expose and to prevent reproduction of gendered inequality within policy and practice. The practices developed were ground breaking, putting gendered power on the map in the governance, design and delivery of public services and employment for the first time as part and parcel of building a new democracy. However, there is a danger that these achievements are lost under the weight of disappointment at failure to dislodge the underlying structures of gender inequality. The vision that we worked towards was grounded in a collective movement for democratic change and this, by its very nature, evoked contestation and political passion that both sustained and constrained our work within the turbulent emotional territory we inhabited and had to negotiate. Re-imagining gender equality was at the core of the vision of the early women's equality work, and we had under-estimated the exhilaration and hostility that this would provoke, and the emotional cost of doing the work. Emotion work (Hochschild, 1983) and relational work (Fletcher 1998), identified by feminist organisation researchers as unrewarded labour that women contribute to organisations, are under-researched dimensions of equality practice, and particularly in these early phases systems to support the work were relatively undeveloped and progress depended on internal and external alliances in a volatile political environment.

In the following chapter our research findings take us into the twenty-first century. Here we find that we are confronted with a paradox: equality practitioners have succeeded in embedding the equality project within business practice in local authorities, but women's equality has all but disappeared within a generic equality discourse. Gender equality was often interpreted as equivalence of need between men and women, and political passion had been replaced by performance standards. This marked the end of a period where there was a fit between explicitly feminist agendas and socialist political institutions committed, however inadequately, to a transformative equality project within the local state. We returned full circle to reliance on political networks to defend institutional mechanisms and forms of promoting equality developed in the context of radical change in the governance and resources available to the local state.

Notes

1 All names have been anonymised.
2 The Greater London Council: see Chapter 3, n.2.
3 The Greater London Authority (GLA) was set up in 2000 as a strategic body to replace the GLC, but with greatly reduced powers and resources.
4 Southall Black Sisters is a collective of South Asian and African-Caribbean women based in London, England.
5 'Sisterhood and After: An Oral History of the Women's Liberation Movement' is a feminist archive housed at the British Library and can be accessed at http://www.bl.uk/learning/histcitizen/sisterhood.

5   Implementing the Gender Equality Duty

Looking through the window of opportunity

In Chapters 3 and 4 we demonstrated how important equality legislation has been in allowing feminists to mobilise the coercive power of the state. Moreover, we have shown that just as crucial as having the right legislation in place is having the political power and will to implement and use it to challenge inequality (Conley, 2013). Researcher and practitioners' accounts in Chapters 3 and 4 signpost the necessarily contested and conflictual nature of equality work, and locates it as an integral dimension of democracy. While the law is necessary to legitimate political initiative, there is a need for committed individuals to 'lead' change, to interpret and translate policy into practice, and make it real.

In Chapter 3 we argued that a particular window of opportunity opened for equality activists in local authorities following the development of legally enforceable equality duties in public authorities. This followed a period of politically led initiatives to promote equality, in which feminists and Left Labour politicians developed processes to support women's participation in democratic decision making and development of services, and redistribute resources more equitably to local communities. The ebbing of political support and changing political and economic climate that coincided with the development of the equality duties led to challenges for independent equality groups and internal equality practitioners when attempting to put the duties into practice. Having the right legislation is, therefore, only one side of the equation. Implementing the law in an effective way and keeping it in place has proved to be as difficult as achieving legislative and organisational change.

In this chapter we draw from our research findings[1] to investigate how far the Gender Equality Duty (GED) made a difference to the development of women's and gender equality work in local government. Based on our empirical research we consider how the subsequent integration of different strands of equality into a single generic equality duty offered both further opportunities and threats to women's equality. The research, conducted in 2008, offers a unique snapshot of how the GED was being implemented in five local authorities in different regions of England during the years leading up to the Equality Act 2010. The five case study local authorities were distinct in their geographical location, political administration, context and history of engagement with feminist organisation. Fifty formal interviews were conducted with key equality actors identified by equalities advisors across the five authorities. These included corporate and service based equality team members, HR managers, trade unionists, independent feminist organisations, senior officers and elected members with responsibility for equality. Two visits were made to each local authority. Our visits were coordinated and hosted by corporate equality advisors, who were invited to comment on our developing analysis in our second visit, and when we had completed the field work. The interview data was supplemented with documentary data analysis and follow-up e-mail correspondence in the years following the research.

Equalities advisors viewed the research as a timely opportunity for more in-depth discussion of the likely impact of a single equalities approach and provided access to key personnel and documents to inform the research. At the time of the research, reviews of the first 12 months of the gender equalities action plans were taking place following the legal requirement in the GED to draw up and publish a scheme based on consultation with 'stakeholders'. By 2008 it was clear that the GED would be merged with the other duties covering race and disability and extended to further strands. The local authorities were, therefore, also considering the case for greater integration across equalities areas.

In the five case studies that follow we introduce the research participants, the practices of gender equality work they had developed and the dilemmas they experienced. Each case study presents a variation on how equality practitioners have engaged with the challenges of promoting gender equality, in their specific context. In the final section we evaluate how the GED made a difference to their practice. Our analysis aims to capture something of the risks and opportunities of doing equality work for those who contributed to our research and what we might understand from their accounts of how and whether the GED has lived up to its transformative potential. In particular, we consider how different approaches to feminist activism and the politics of difference are played out in the delivery of public services.

Case study 1: Modernisation and mainstreaming: gender equality by performance management

Our first case study local authority is a city that describes itself as having, in the last 20 years, transformed itself from being mainly a producer of industrial goods into a broad based commercial centre. The population is diverse, and includes over 130 nationalities. At the time of our visit the city employed approximately 35,000 people, either directly or indirectly and the political administration of the authority was led by a coalition of the Conservatives and Liberal Democrats. Between 2004 and 2011 elections had resulted in no overall control. From 1980 to 2004 the council was under Labour control.

The authority had embraced a 'New Public Management' approach and a business plan was the core of the organisational strategy. In the business plan, interconnectivity and partnership working, equality, cohesion, integration and sustainability were identified as key themes. The business plan made reference to ongoing organisation change and capacity building in order to improve outcomes for 'customers' and achieve 'smarter working: better results'. Commitment to employee engagement, increasing equality and valuing the diversity of all communities in the city were stated objectives alongside partnership with organisations that collectively provided services for the city.

The equality and diversity strategy was launched two years before our visit. Its aims were to identify, remove and diminish barriers to services and employment across all equality strands. Community cohesion, defined as 'raising awareness and understanding, breaking down barriers, developing shared values, mutual respect and trust', was described as integral to the Council plan and included as a dimension of impact assessments. To support the strategy, information documents had been developed for staff, including detailed guidance for equality monitoring and diversity along with cohesion impact assessments. The council had achieved level 3 of the Equality Standard (see Chapter 3), and was working towards level 4.[2]

At the time of our first visit, the local authority employed a corporate equalities team of 18 and, following reorganisation five years before, was in the process of a major restructuring to consolidate business planning processes. The work and organisation of the equalities unit had significantly changed, embracing performance management and rejecting a politically driven 'adversarial' approach to equalities work developed in previous years under Labour administrations. Indeed, most of the team members had a background in performance management and eschewed earlier approaches to equality practice in local government.

> At that time [1990s] the equalities team was very confrontational and I think that was a traditional equality team in many ways … it was very much – you will do this, this is the right way forward – it was a fight. I think there were some positives about that, the passion, the commitment, there were a lot of things moved forward … but also it turned a lot of people off. So it left a lot of people behind.
>
> (Corporate equalities advisor)

> I've worked for the council for such a long time and I had experience where I would never have rung the equality team … because I think people in equalities have often been seen as politically correct which is awful!
>
> (Corporate equalities team member)

Equality practice in this local authority looked very different to the municipal feminism discussed in Chapter 3 and the early phases of equality work described in Chapter 4, but it was clear that the underlying principles of harnessing the power of both the national and local state were still visible. The corporate equality team had mobilised the GED to create an elaborate architecture to support and embed equality and gender mainstreaming within business planning processes. They had harnessed discourses of modernisation embedded in major reorganisations of public services, driven by national Labour government agendas, to develop and embed outcome focused systems for performance management of equality and diversity within a discourse of service quality. In line with these changes, the internal organisation of the equalities team had changed so that team member's roles were no longer equality strand specific, but generic and based on departmental functions. In order to comply with the legislative requirement to consult, a system of strand specific employee forums and community hubs were planned to enable employees, communities and service users to contribute to this process.

These changes had been motivated partly in anticipation of the merging of the separate equality duties into a single duty that integrated all equality strands:

> What we did at the time was to look at a better way of organising ourselves, which fitted organisationally but also fitted with what we could see was happening in future legislation.
>
> (Corporate equalities advisor)

However legislation was not the only driver for embedding quality into performance management and business planning. The equality team had mobilised external benchmarking systems for local government and the Equality Standard and Framework (see Chapters 3 and 4) to embed equality into systems for improving the quality of services they delivered. They stressed that the reward of getting an externally recognised badge was a more powerful motivator than sanctions associated with legal compliance.

> We have a number of drivers helping us, but also ... the sense that [the local authority] does want to improve, does want to be the best it can be to customers and staff ...
>
> As an organisation we like to have levels to achieve and things to strive for and I think the framework kind of helps us do that, it helps to progress the agenda in that way.
>
> (Corporate equalities advisor)

Their strategy was double layered, building equality architecture for reward and compliance, and then 'building ownership' within service directorates to translate equality and diversity principles into their own service planning (Page and Conley, 2010). While this aspect of the strategy was designed to reduce resistance to equal opportunity policy and practice (Jewson and Mason, 1986), it also tapped into service managers' desire to deliver a good quality service (Newman, 2002). To achieve this, equalities advisors became experts in facilitating development of a gender lens for managers within HR and service departments (Page and Conley, 2010), an approach that practitioners in Chapter 4 had described as achieving 'perceptual shift'.

> We are very clear that the directorates own the issues, ... and that needs to be based on what as an organisation we're trying to achieve and what our communities are telling us they want us to achieve ... at the end of the day

the directorates have to be clear about what they have to achieve, how they are doing to do that, how they know when they have got there.

(Corporate equalities advisor)

I have attended meetings where all the members of staff at different levels have actually flagged up issues and been quite vocal about that and clear about what the issues are and keen to make a difference. Well that certainly makes me smile, it makes me think that's one of the reasons we are here.

(Corporate equalities team member)

Equality and diversity policy within business planning documents was defined in terms of fairness, equal access to services and employment and elimination of barriers, and creating an environment in which 'all people are respected and valued' (Equality and Diversity Policy, 2008–11). Documents referred to equality, diversity and community cohesion impact assessments. Examples of successful gender equality outcomes given by participants referred to tailoring to meet women's specific needs where they had previously been overlooked, such as breastfeeding facilities for women accessing services, addressing teenage pregnancy within services for NEETS,[3] and inter-agency domestic violence training for policy, education and childcare workers throughout the city. While these examples might be said to reinforce women's traditional roles rather than deconstructing gender relations, they also illustrate how gender mainstreaming challenged managers to imagine the specificity and reality of a wide range of women's lives, to consult and to seek out research data that would help them understand what women might need to access existing services and what additional services would address their specific needs and priorities:

There's an expectation that services, either within the council or their external partners will address equality and diversity in their [children's services] work.

(Departmental equalities advisor)

In this sense the GED was used to open a space for considering what it might mean to 'gender' the discourse and practice of service planning. Encouraging and enabling use of creative imagination, as a means of engaging with gender difference, emerged as a theme towards the end of our discussions in interviews.

In response to our questions about the risks of managers adopting a tick box approach to equalities impact assessments, corporate equalities advisors spoke of their invitation to managers to put together narrative accounts of what they had set out to achieve, to illustrate how equality targets would improve service quality. These accounts of a 'conversational approach', akin to coaching, to encourage creative engagement with process and to 'mainstream' equality into the discourse of quality, lay alongside and underpinned their detailed accounts of process and procedure for compliance and measuring performance. Whilst they demonstrated potential for radical engagement with gendered assumptions, this was limited by the discourses of gender available to the actors involved, and the practical priorities of service users.

> People are driven by different things aren't they? We will use absolutely every tool available. But also it's really important to be able to de-mystify the thing about equality and diversity so that it's not about saying the right or wrong thing in every situation. It's about enabling people to have those discussions and then take it from there.
>
> (Corporate equalities advisor)

> We are able to support them [service managers], equip them with the tools to do what they need to do and to look at what the equality and diversity issues might be and those inequalities, but also to help them make the connection with the bigger picture, that vision.
>
> (Corporate equalities advisor)

Equalities advisors effectively described a process of reframing quality, so as to place a consideration of gender difference and diversity associated with the equality strands in the legislation (gender, race, disability, sexuality, age, religion and belief) at the heart of the notion of 'quality' service. The knowledge base needed to engage with this reframing of 'quality' could, they felt, come from experience of delivering front line services to diverse communities. Thus in their view the experience of being providers of service tailored to diverse community needs, rather than the movement politics of a previous era, provided the knowledge base that could inform gender mainstreaming and equality practice:

> It's about recognising ... people are not as unknowledgeable as it is kind of perceived sometimes. You know, you're a frontline service provider, you understand what the issues are, you've got people coming in making comments and issues are being raised ... most of us have come from service delivery at some point so we have that experience ...
>   It then means that people are responsible you know, it's not just the equality team, we're not fonts of all absolute knowledge around the areas. But we do have a way of teasing out what those issues are.
>
> (Corporate equalities team advisor)

Although service equality advisors described their approach to mainstreaming equality as 'iron fist in velvet glove', it was by no means always a smooth process. Progress was uneven, some managers more open than others. Therefore recognising the limits of what could be achieved was important.

> We encourage and we corral you know, iron fist in velvet glove stuff. ... It's been really quite interesting and quite challenging working with some of those chief officers to help them understand how this agenda relates to the services [leisure, economic services, transport, planning]. Sometimes it's

very tangential, and then for other services it's absolutely central to everything they do. I think we've learned that and know where to put the balance of our efforts. We're not going to knock our heads against brick walls with people for whom it's always going to be quite limited.

(Departmental equalities advisor)

One of the problems of locating equality within a business case that appeals to service managers is that cost is always at the forefront of the argument. The strongest illustration of this point is that equal pay for women employees was one of the most contentious issues in this and all our local authorities. Just as gender mainstreaming equality was achieved by harnessing equality to 'quality', so equal pay was achieved by harnessing gender equality to the introduction of 'single status', a national collective agreement with trade unions to harmonise the pay of manual and white collar workers and the job evaluation required to achieve this (Webb, 2001; Conley, 2013). Through several years of difficult negotiations with trade unions culminating in many thousands of legal cases, significant pay rises had been achieved for some of the lowest paid women workers in most local authorities. Despite a pay reduction for some manual workers in traditionally male dominated jobs we found that a sense of positive achievement rather than of embattlement seemed to have won out:

We've implemented a new pay structure, we've changed the rates of pay for thousands of employees and we have a pay structure, which meets the equal pay challenge going forward. That's something that everybody who's been involved in is proud of because that has a very tangible effect on for example females paid in jobs that are the lowest in the pay structure.

(HR manager)

Performance indicators, reward systems and legal requirements were powerful drivers, in the absence of vocal local feminist organisation that typified the municipal feminism of earlier periods. However, the absence of a specific feminist advocacy also meant loss of critical content brought to processes for mainstreaming gender into services. Access to data was limited, and interpretation dependent on service managers' knowledge and understanding of diversity and gender difference. Managers sometimes drew from the life experience of colleagues, but there was no evidence of political commitment in how this was understood or analysed:

You are often relying on people's own imagination in terms of understanding the issues. Now we work with a woman in the Early Years service who happens to be a lesbian herself and has two adopted children and she sees the potential issues facing single parents, gay families, etc.

(Departmental equalities advisor)

Performance drivers were both a help and a hindrance in this respect, offering opportunities for critical reflection and learning, but also potential for a routinised, technocratic, 'tick box' approach to equality. Service organisations were sometimes required to meet conflicting performance targets and this hindered gender mainstreaming outcomes. One example we were given was where the police were required to demonstrate investigation of complaints on domestic violence whilst the Crown Prosecution Service was required to demonstrate successful prosecutions and so would not seek to pursue cases, such as domestic violence, with a high attrition rate.

A skilful combination of these approaches was difficult to find but it had been achieved in some instances. Our discussions with the manager of the domestic violence project provided a very good illustration of effective use of the GED by the harnessing of performance management. The following mini case study offers a positive example to illustrate the potential of the GED to effect feminist change.

Mini case study: a multi-agency domestic violence partnership

M is employed by the local authority to lead a multi-agency project team to ensure a citywide domestic violence project is delivered. The team is made up of local authority staff and is located in the community safety division of neigh-bourhood and communities. The project was set up to comply with legislation on crime reduction that required local authorities to form partnerships with police to tackle crime and disorder and community safety. The project had drawn up a domestic violence strategy for the city, in partnership with a wide range of organisations and council departments, including children's ser-vices, housing and human resources, local women's refuges and independent organisations. Linked in to national domestic violence networks and policy, the case study illustrates how it was possible to successfully and skilfully negotiate liberal and transformative discourses of gender equality, and alongside this how the performance culture and compliance with legislation provided the leverage necessary to make change.

M stressed that domestic violence is primarily about male violence against women and children, and that while this principle underpinned every part of their work, expressing this as a stance made them vulnerable to attack:

> This is about patriarchy really and the way society is set up … so that underpins every single piece of work we do, whether it's going to talk to a women's group, deliver training to senior managers or commission a service … That can make us vulnerable to being seen as man hating and all the rest of it so what we have to make clear is that any good practice that's developed should benefit male victims as well and more research needs to happen around male victims and same sex relationships.

In this case the strategic approach was to adopt a liberal, symmetrical public face for the project. Surprisingly, M found the police receptive to a feminist approach because they see the day-to-day impact of domestic violence and because of their 'control and command' culture:

> The culture of the police is that they have a can do approach and if their managers tell them to do something or think in a certain way, they will just do it. That's the beauty of working with police officers. I'm lucky enough to be working at a superintendent level with police officers who are *au fait* with working in partnership ... and receptive to thinking the issue through with us. Also because police are going to be attending incidents and they see that it's overwhelmingly men doing horrendous things to women and children they don't have an issue with us approaching it that way.

M describes how she works the tension between liberal and transformative discourses of gendered power in how the GED was interpreted:

> By being pragmatic I think. We use terms and terminology interchangeably. If we're sat round a table with the police, you know, we talk in a more gender neutral way. But actually, the more we've done that, the more the police have become receptive to thinking through the issue. In actual fact, the police are probably less resistant than some of the other organisations ... They are thinking the gender equality duty is all about treating everybody equally, even if it's not a level playing field to begin with.

M gives many examples of how the project has harnessed the performance culture successfully to create spaces where awareness is raised of gendered power and practices developed to address this:

> At the moment there's a quality assurance framework that all childcare providers work to and it's quite prestigious to have it, everybody's working to it.

The framework created a multi-agency accredited training programme with health, housing, children's services and midwives where detailed work is done on understanding gendered power and how to work with it in practice.

A 'minimum standards quality mark' was used to do an annual health check with organisations to make sure that all staff are trained and have up-to-date information. M stressed that important leverage was provided by having nationally recognised accreditation for their training or a link to formal qualification on professional development, national targets or performance indicators. Despite this, levels of take up were uneven and whether action on domestic violence was seen as mainstream or marginal was still dependent on individual commitment at senior level.

The business case was not easy to make because, when attention was drawn to domestic violence, a previously invisible problem is revealed with the potential for a significant draw on resources. However, sometimes significant resource allocation was made simply because senior managers wanted it:

> So the only way I think we've got that is because we've got people in positions who are saying, yes it's important and we need to do it.

M spoke of the pitfalls and advantages of activism of the late 1980s and 1990s, as a strategy for addressing intersectionality (see Chapters 2 and 3):

> We used to have a whole black women's faction if you like to our work, whereas what we do now is integrate and embed race into our service plan every year. For six years we had an officer who worked solely on disabled women's issues, again we've really just embedded and tried to mainstream plans for disabled women.

M saw this shift away from reliance on external lobbying to address intersectional concerns as a positive move, towards a more consistent and strategic approach at senior level. The loss of knowledge and expertise that went with the loss of specific resources within the equality team did not appear to be an issue, perhaps because as a black feminist she embodied intersectionality and maintained the links with external networks.

Both the case study authority and the mini case study illustrate how it was possible to successfully and skilfully negotiate liberal and transformative discourses of gender equality within a multi-agency partnership. Compliance with legislation, including the GED, and the performance culture provided the necessary leverage to engage practitioners with change. However, in the context of predominantly liberal discourses of gender, clear transformative values and principles held by senior committed individuals were necessary to assert the transformative potential of the GED. An important casualty of this approach was the risk of losing the resource to engage with the distinctive needs of different groups of women.

The narratives of the corporate equality advisors strongly suggested that the predominant discourse of quality, and the culture of constant improvement supported by performance management, provided an environment favourable to outcome focused gender equality work. The language of quality and performance supplied a politically neutral and media friendly discourse for equality change. Their work was no longer associated with externally imposed political and feminist agendas, but rather a shared desire to make a difference. Yet they also stated that compliance with legislation and audit frameworks were essential levers.

These narratives suggested that the external political and legal environment did shape strategy, but did not determine it. Equalities advisors saw themselves as developing strategy, and processes, that prefigured equality legislation and were adapted to the direction of flow, for example, streamlining equality impact assessments, and moving away from strand specific to generic assessments.

Category based equality had been abandoned as a basis for organisation of the equality team and was seen as limiting and not adapted to the intersectionality of women's lived experience, or to the changes in legislation. Moving with the times, reading the political landscape and adapting equalities practice to constantly evolving organising processes was key to their strategy for gender mainstreaming and for addressing intersectionality, if not always the politics of difference.

Gender mainstreaming required skilful mobilisation of legal compliance alongside 'soft skills' of negotiation and facilitation. Sophisticated readings of organisational and professional cultures, and capacity to translate across discourses of equality and of service quality, were levers for achieving buy in. The key to success, as described in these accounts, was the shift from being prescriptive, imposing an externally defined political agenda, from being 'thought police', to building ownership from within a predominant organisation culture and discourse.

Whilst it was clear to us that the business case served as a distancing strategy from an earlier, more radical, approach to equalities work because it was considered more effective for gaining consensual change, it was also clear that without political support and leadership, the approach was problematic. In a second round of restructuring following a change of leadership, the equality team told us that the future of the corporate equality unit was uncertain, with potential dispersal of team members within directorates, retaining a single senior representative on the corporate management team. When we contacted them some months after the end of the research project, we found that the equalities team had indeed been disbanded, leaving their former manager as an equality champion on the corporate management team, but without an equality team to support her. Despite this, and as a result of their work, the local authority had reached the highest level of achievement on the Equality Standard for local government.

Case study 2: Feminist leadership, precarious progress: from feminist social justice to privatisation and outsourcing

Our second case study is a city with a strong industrial history and tradition of labour and feminist movement. The local authority is a major employer in the city with, at the time of our visit, more than 18,000 employees, including all state school staff. Its publicity claims that after a long period of decline, the local economy is undergoing a revival as a city of commerce. The population was growing in diversity, with around 16 per cent from black and ethnic minority groups. For much of its history the council had been led by Labour councillors and was noted for its Leftist sympathies. However, the Liberal Democrats controlled the council between 1999 and 2001 and took control again in 2008 at the time of our research.

The Victorian town hall seemed to tell a story of past industry and prosperity, its sculpted frieze depicting labour movement struggles in the steel works, and marble interior telling a story of civic pride and wealth long gone. One of our interviewees expressed continuity between her work and this history of labour movement, referring to her being the third generation of female family members to participate in labour and feminist movements. However, in contrast to the confidence in the business planning approach of the first case study, this authority was filled with a sense of a precarious and uncertain future for feminist gender equality work. Following a change of local political administration, a massive programme of outsourcing services and privatisation was underway, and internal relations were being transformed by the introduction of business planning through major restructuring. The local authority and its approach to equalities work was in transition, from a consultative, bottom up strand-specific approach grounded in a long history of social and trade union movement, to a business focused corporate approach into which gender equality was to be mainstreamed. The organisation as a whole was suffering from change fatigue, reeling from the impact of these profound changes in culture and ethos of governance, democracy and of public service.

This local authority equalities team is considerably smaller than Case Study 1, with a corporate equalities unit of four, and part time equalities advisors in service directorates. The future of the team and location of equalities work was under discussion at the time of our research interviews. The fears and scepticism about the fate of equalities we encountered during our research were well founded as the equality unit has, as in Case Study 1, since been disbanded and officers relocated in departments with no specific equalities brief.

The recent change from a Labour to a Liberal Democrat political administration had introduced radical change in the ethos of the organisation, equalities discourse, resourcing and organisation. The equalities unit was seeking ways to shape and sustain equality practice within the transition towards a more business-based environment. The changes were gathering momentum and the direction of travel was marketisation of public services, privatisation, outsourcing of services and radical internal reorganisation on the basis of business principles. This not only changed organisational roles and job titles, but introduced market principles as a basis for relationships between services and departments. There are clear similarities in the restructuring of equalities work that we report in Case Study 1, but the striking difference between the equalities teams in the two authorities was their attitude to these changes. In our second case study authority the team displayed a far more critical analysis:

> The whole organisation has been basically swamped by change and people have got change fatigue ... it's one of the biggest privatisation programmes running ...
>
> We are having to move things around and change the language of things to fit in with the new administration.
>
> (Corporate equalities advisor)

Team members described how the change in political administration and restructuring was accompanied by a discursive shift from 'equality of outcome' to 'equal opportunities', a move towards generic job descriptions and an intention to reduce specialist resources. Equality was to be 'mainstreamed' from the corporate centre through 'business partnerships' with service departments and it was anticipated that the equalities team would be replaced by corporate 'business partners' who were leading the business transformation restructure, and who spoke of 'selling' equality to service departments in order to standardise practice. This move towards a more generic, business based approach to promoting equality coincided with a recent loss of interest in women's equality and an increasing focus on men's issues in service provision – particularly in health, housing and education:

> We had a women's unit and officers working specifically on women's equality issues in employment and service delivery. We did a lot of very good work but things have changed and evolved and with things like flexible working and childcare we are no longer arguing from a feminist perspective but from a gender perspective. It's whether people pick up that it's a women's or a gender issue which is problematic I think.
>
> There's been quite a forceful argument about providing more services for men who are victims of domestic abuse. That's quite problematic in that services for women are nowhere near what we would like them to be … But it was councillors saying; well shouldn't we have equal services?
>
> (Corporate equalities advisor)

The more critical and reflective approach to the implementation of business principles in this case study was evident in considerations of implementing an integrated equality duty. The equalities team was apprehensive about losing gains they had made in the context of a new local political authority leadership that was demonstrating a reduced interest in equality. They were proud of the work they had done in establishing separate forums for employees focusing on a range of equality strands, but they were also aware of the challenges this posed for developing understanding of the intersections between inequalities.

EQUALITY TEAM LEADER: 'So whilst we think that we have made good progress on that, we're now concerned that those forums are very narrow. They focus on their specific issues.'

INTERVIEWER: 'So black women, for example, don't speak up … '

EQUALITY TEAM LEADER: 'They might speak about race, but they wouldn't necessarily speak about gender and race. That's an issue for us about how we tackle that, because we've got something that's quite positive and that's quite valued in the organisation, but we sort of need it now to look a little bit broader and how we tackle that, we've got to sort of work that through, haven't we, because we wouldn't want to take any action that would seem to be taking apart what we've spent a long time setting up. But we just need to take it to another level now to ask people to start to think about equalities in a wider context, rather than specific issues.

An example of what intersectionality might mean in practice and some of the contradictions it could raise came from the local authority translation and interpretation service, working in partnership with the private sector to provide face to face, telephone and written access to services in 170 languages to the city's multi-ethnic community. In discussion with us, the project manager reflected on the challenges of balancing sensitivity to cultural and individual values with the council's commitment to promoting equality and diversity. Engaging with intersectionality was a core issue for the project. She emphasised, for example, that they catered for preference for female or male interpreters in each of the languages provided. Clashes of value were dealt with firmly and with an aim to achieve resolution. To illustrate this, she described how she had taken time to help an interpreter they employed to understand that supporting lesbian and gay members of the community was part of his job and that his faith could not be allowed to prevent him from providing an interpretation service for a young person suffering discrimination.

In contrast with our first case study, there were many references to illustrate the important leadership role of individual feminist women in management and in the trade union. Their commitment was a means to access feminist knowledge content and to sustain a women's equality agenda in a context of reduced political commitment to women's equality work:

> I think it definitely helps ... that my service manager is really committed ... if we raised a concern where we don't think she should sign it [an equalities impact assessment] off then she would back us up on that or help us to come up with a diplomatic solution, or we do the development work afterwards.
>
> (Departmental equalities advisor)

Advisors spoke of their efforts to work alongside service managers to improve the quality of equality impact assessments, to develop 'smarter' performance targets and more robust processes for accountability, towards a more effective focus on outcomes. Their view was that this leadership role needed to be held by a dedicated specialist team of committed equalities advisors and could not be adequately replaced by the generic business consultants who were designated responsible in the new regime.

> If you just all became generic policy officers eventually when you recruit ... they're not going to have the same commitment. It's just a target and it will be just something they do. There are some things you just have to be committed to.
>
> (Corporate equalities team member)

An important external source of support for the equality advisors was a strong, well established local network of women in lead roles across agencies in the locality. An independent women's trust had been formed out of a council led women's forum 10 years previously. Made up of researchers and activists and local women's organisations in the region, the trust had links to national organisations, including the Women's National Commission,[4] and well-established national feminist organisations such as Women in Manual Trades. The women's officer in the main trade union branch was a key player in the implementation and development of women's equality policy and practice and a participant in the independent network. There were close informal links between these external networks and equalities advisors. Frequent references were made to their importance and to the role of individual feminist senior managers, in sustaining women's equality work within the local authority, in the context of political change:

> We would not have had that gender duty event with the chief executive and leader of the council speaking had Joanne not pushed that as the Lord Mayor ... Joanne, when she was Lord Mayor, worked for the local newspaper to organise a big women's award event for services to public life and business. It was a bit like the Oscars! You see, it's very dependent on individuals really.
>
> (Corporate equalities advisor)

> Our new assistant chief executive is keen to go for the Equality Framework. She's also keen to do more work around gender issues, which we feel we've not been doing very much of in recent times. ... We're setting up a new strategic group that she is going to chair and she expects senior managers to be involved in that group. ... .So from a position of thinking we were going to have it taken away from us and it was going to be mainstreamed, which in a lot of peoples' views meant people wouldn't do it, she's now trying to set up systems to ensure that people accept the responsibilities for doing the work as part and parcel of what they do. We will be there in the wings sort of doing bits, but not as a core team.
>
> (Corporate equalities advisor)

While the presence of strong feminist managers was repeatedly referred to as a critical factor, so was the precariousness of relying on them:

> They've got a manager, Sue, who's incredibly good on equality issues, but you know there's only so many hours in the day and she's completely overworked ... senior managers have completely changed, every single senior manager has changed within the past year.
>
> (Corporate equalities advisor)

> Obviously there are some committed people who will do just because they are committed. But that certainly isn't the majority of people ... in the case of equality what makes it work or doesn't work sometimes is around strong personalities, who are committed to the work. If they go, that can leave a gap.
>
> (Corporate equalities advisor)

The worrying thing for trade unions is you can have the best policies in the world but if people don't know that they're going to be policed in operating them, there's no pressure on them to do anything.

> (Trade union women's group chair and
> trade union convenor for women in the region)

Equalities advisors had lobbied for a strong corporate strategic lead to maintain the equality agenda within the restructured organisation. In the context of the push to make massive savings and privatisation, address inconsistency across departments, and introduce smarter targets they spoke of working more selectively and strategically. This meant targeting areas where they could make a difference and working with partners to 'get robust data so we can challenge the myths and challenge where the gaps are' (Corporate equalities advisor).

While there had been successful external lobbying to maintain strand specific equality fora for disability and ethnic minority communities, there was resistance to an equivalent forum for women, and an assumption that gender equality had been 'done' evidenced by representation of women at senior level:[5]

> I think not all women see things from the perspective of women, as you know. But because these women are in positions of power, there may well be a view that women have a certain amount of power within the city. Therefore you don't need to create a process that means more women would need to be involved.
>
> (Senior manager)

Implementation of equal pay, as in Case Study 1, had been conflicted and difficult, contributing to low morale caused by major organisational change. Negotiations had been long, drawn out over 10 years, and a pay and grading exercise was just arriving at a conclusion. There was a sense that this was too contentious an issue to discuss in any detail with us as researchers, but there was hope that negotiations had arrived at an acceptable conclusion.

Our research participants in Case Study 2 felt that the new political administration had only shown commitment to the equality agenda when they became aware that the local authority would be measured and assessed on the basis of compliance with equality legislation:

> You've come at quite an interesting time really, because we don't know where it's going to go. Now I don't know what's been said politically … they started off saying that they weren't going to have any equalities department at all, but I think now they've got in and they realise they'd got to do some … management of it. I think they're recognising there is a need clearly because they're going to be measured against things, but it's how robust it is, is what we need to wait and see … the difficulty is the effects of it could be quite long term rather than short term change.
>
> (Trade union women's group chair and
> convenor for women in the region)

As in Case Study 1, equalities team members offered many examples of how they had skilfully harnessed equality to predominant performance discourses and created structures around community consultation to promote women's equality. There were several statements of how important it was to embed women's equality within other, more mainstream discourses but, unlike Case Study 1, there was a sense of loss that 'as a thing in itself' gender equality was no longer considered a credible goal.

> I don't know if you agree, but I think that as soon as gender is just seen as a thing on its own, then it loses its usefulness. It's when it is seen as something that is part of procurement, part of employment in the authority, part of education, that it becomes meaningful ... you know, people don't want just courses for women about women these days. You know what I mean? It's got to be for a purpose these days.
>
> (Corporate equality advisor)

In these accounts the business narrative and references to willingness to learn, building ownership and incremental progress, lay alongside a more oppositional narrative of the need for stronger scrutiny, for coercion and sanctions. Narratives of incremental progress through learning were juxtaposed with references to feminist advocacy, in which gender equality mainstreaming was contested, achieved through local democratic process and uneven progress. The progress narratives offered tidier, more sanitised approaches that masked the messiness and contested nature of building commitment through committed leadership, the real work of promoting women's and gender equality in a context of phenomenal workloads, change fatigue and massive attack on ethos of public service.

In our conversations with equalities team members there was a sense of continuity with a history of feminist and trade union working-class organisation in a local industrial past. This was manifest through reference to the key role played by individual feminist and committed individual women in leadership roles within the local authority and externally, linking with local and national gender equality advocacy networks, often formed out the mass industrial conflict of the 1980s. It contrasted starkly with Case Study 1, where the history of working-class or movement organisation for equality had already been discarded and disowned.

Our interviews conveyed a sense of a preferred regime that was fading. Pride in a history of solidarity and shared feminist vision, of advocacy and of bottom up participative democracy that were losing ground in the new regime and sadness at its potential loss was palpable. The equality team members felt they had much to be proud of yet conveyed a sense of vulnerability to negative judgement within the new regime. There was an acute awareness of the precariousness of the equality project and a feeling that the feminist movement was under attack by the new political administration. Our research conversations captured a moment of transition from an explicitly socialist and feminist ethos of redistributive justice, towards marketisation of public services and business transformation driven by national government but also by a newly elected local political administration. The scale and speed of change was described as 'massive' and compliance had been essential to protect equalities work in the new business regime. In this context, the work of gender and equality mainstreaming meant translating a feminist vision of collective and social equality into the new organisational discourse of service improvement and customer service. A shift from equality of outcome to equality of opportunity was accompanied by a drift from the collective to the individual and, in this sense, from transformational potential to liberal equality – a return to 'tinkering' with some 'tailoring' (Rees, 1998). Within this scenario, there was also a sense of waning commitment to women or gender equality, and a sense that the presence of senior women in leadership roles in the city meant there was no further need for action on gender equality. On the other hand, supportive senior women offered leadership that could provide potential for meaningful gender equality outcomes.

In this context of reduced commitment to resourcing of women's equality work within the local authority political administration, two factors seemed vital to sustain potential for a transformational dimension for gender mainstreaming. Equality legislation and national audit benchmarking instruments assumed more importance to protect and to sustain commitment to the gender equality agenda. As in Case Study 1, equalities advisors referred to the GED as a key instrument, but not the engine of this process. Indeed they considered that their equality practice was well in advance of the legislation, prefiguring it in many ways, during a favourable local political regime. Now that local political priorities threatened to undermine this work, compliance and the equality duties assumed greater importance to legitimise, protect and sustain the work of mainstreaming women's equality, within the business transformation agenda.

In summary, external networks of advocates for women's equality, including independent activists and organisations, trade unions and local government practitioners, both local and national, sustained the work within the local authority. They did so by creating opportunities for knowledge exchange leading to the development of strategy and practice. In this, a sense of history and of continuity in being part of a collectively held on-going project was key. Feminist leadership was dispersed across organisations and networks within a field of activity. An organisational culture and processes that enabled and affirmed links with and participation in the policy process by local communities had been part of this history. It was hoped this would be sustained within the new customer focus, although this was based on individual, and not collective, priorities or needs.

Case study 3: Belief not duty: leading gender equality and diversity within partnerships and with local communities

Our third case study is an inner London local authority, with a diverse population, which is 34 per cent black and minority ethnic. Its political administration has been consistently Labour. At the time of our research it employed approximately 10,000 staff including those working in schools. This London local authority was the first to set up a women's equality committee and team, and the first, in the 1970s, to develop work on equal pay for work of equal value, which had later contributed to new legislation. Of all our case studies, it had the longest track record of women's equality work, had achieved the highest level of the Equality Standard, and was the most sophisticated in terms of integration of explicit commitment to equality and diversity within its corporate strategy.

Equality work was led by a corporate management board (CMB), made up of executive directors one of whom, as equality 'champion', held a corporate equality and diversity leadership brief. The CMB was chaired by the head of a corporate policy and performance team, where generic equalities advisors were located. Equality impact assessments were drawn up by directorates, with support from the corporate equalities advisors, and signed off by the CMB. There was a small corporate equality team with generic equality briefs and they were located centrally in a 'policy and partnership' unit.

This was the only local authority where we were invited to interview executive directors with corporate responsibility for equalities work, as well as equalities advisors. These were the chair of the corporate equalities board, the corporate equalities 'champion', the head of human resources and a corporate equalities advisor. Their narratives conveyed a consistently optimistic picture of gender equality work, building on a history of leading the field on equalities in public services. Each of our interviewees referred with pride to the history of initiating women's equality work in the local authority in the 1970s, embracing these 'historic events' as a core dimension of the present. There had been continuity in commitment to equality and diversity from political leaders, and their leadership was exercised in partnership with voluntary organisations, local community organisations and local service providers. The equality and diversity agenda was described as led by external events and local community leadership that, in contrast to our other case studies, had and continued to be embraced by the local authority:

> History has been a teacher of institutions and there has been a contribution from our community responding to a series of historic events and experiences that shape the sort of organisation we are … that's why I started with the 1970s – the women's working party and the race working party – at a time when other institutions were really struggling with the agendas. So some of our political leaders, some of our community leaders have significantly influenced the institutions sufficiently that we've been able to make quicker progress than some institutions because they haven't had that support in the community.
>
> (Chair of CEB, Head of Policy and Performance)

The local authority considered itself to be a model employer and service provider, with national influence and profile, presenting many examples of strategies designed to achieve maximum impact to promote women's equality. To close the gender pay gap political decisions were taken to reject strategies such as outsourcing that would achieve legal compliance and be less costly than employing women in senior jobs:

> Since the equal pay legislation ... society has come to value the caring professions a little bit more ... We need to decide as an employer whether we want to be at the forefront of that change that we want to create in society or not, and we decided we wanted to be at the forefront of it ...
>
> To be honest, my role is about promoting [the Borough] as a great place to work. I will use whatever influence I've got nationally to do so and I will do so particularly to target potentially senior women because ... we've got an untapped resource and it brings us success.
>
> (Head of HR)

The political leadership of this local authority was closely associated with New Labour and had fully embraced the modernisation agenda. Services were increasingly delivered through partnerships with external service providers and the local authority took a lead role in developing structures and processes to promote and support equalities strategy, work with partner organisations and to collect the necessary data to construct an evidence base:

> An evidence base that establishes the nature of discrimination and dis-advantage that prevails and continues to prevail and the whole weight of the partnership is working towards addressing that in all its complex array.
>
> (Chair of CEB, Head of Policy and Performance)

Gender and women's equality issues within a variety of policy and service areas were specifically addressed on the basis of 'reducing the gap on a national average', for example, in health outcomes. The examples given were of issues traditionally associated with women – smoking, teenage pregnancy, healthy eating for mothers and domestic violence. Only one discordant note within this optimistic narrative was struck by the corporate equalities team member, suggesting a more conflicted picture from those at the front line of doing gender equality work and reminiscent of the critique of earlier equalities work in our first case study:

> I am not the equalities police, so don't think I am going to be on your back about stuff if I don't need to be.
>
> (Corporate equalities advisor)

While it was clear that the approach to equality and diversity work was performance led and couched within the 'business case' for equality, each interviewee defined the core business of the organisation as serving a diverse local community. Reference was made to a national profile for work done around gender and planning reported in the national press and an academic publication (Burgess, 2008). Diversity was a resource, within local communities and within the establishment of employees, most of whom it was stressed lived locally and, therefore, had a strong sense of what discrimination and disadvantage meant to residents. There was reference to senior managers who were passionately committed to specific equality agendas, including strong representation of senior women.

In policy terms this translated into the use of single strand-specific equality schemes alongside a generic comprehensive equality plan:

> We've been on a journey some other local authorities have been on. Producing a comprehensive equalities scheme ... [Our approach] has allowed us to look at some of the cross between issues that affect no one specific equality group but across equalities. ... but also made sure that single equalities issues were still recognised and inputted into the council. It means we've been able to have a more mature dialogue with the community ... the single equalities bill will maintain that momentum for us.
>
> (Chair of CEB, Head of Policy and Performance)

There was, therefore, a belief that the problems of intersectionality and the politics of difference were being addressed. The generic and single duty anticipated in new legislation was embraced as enabling greater flexibility and work with inter-sections across equality strands but, as in Case Study 2, a single equalities approach was not seen as an alternative to addressing multiple and separate inequalities. Merging equality strands and their representative bodies was con-sidered to be a national government policy trend that the local authority was prepared to resist:

> Nobody wants to buy into 'let's do away with all our single equalities organisations and have a one overriding equalities organisation' ... I think around single equalities people feel there's too much at stake, there's too much to be developed, there's too much we want to hold onto.
>
> (Chair of CEB, Head of Policy and Performance)

Legal compliance was seen as a useful and necessary instrument, but also, as in Case Studies 1 and 2, posing dangers and limitations. Commitment to equality and diversity was felt by the senior managers we interviewed to be embedded at the core of the local authority culture, regardless of legislation, and any change in local political commitment to equality was unthinkable:

> Clearly there's an important responsibility that we have to ensure the organisation is fully aware of its duties and responsibilities ... but these are not things that are prescribed to use in the context in which we come to the equalities agenda. It's an understanding of what's right in terms of delivery of service and support to our communities in relation to equalities more broadly.
>
> In terms of our respective duties, about keeping the organisation informed and up to date in terms of its statutory responsibilities ... our

commitment to the agenda comes from more than that. It comes from actually believing.

(Equalities champion)

It was striking that the senior equalities lead at executive level was totally committed to creating a culture in which the business case for equality and diversity was defined in terms of community needs, with compliance as an ultimate safety net:

> What you really ought to be investing in as well as to support the law is actually investing in that culture that generates the business case … understanding your community and delivering to that community's best needs.
>
> (Equalities champion)

Yet she also recognised that ensuring that staff developed the outlook and practice necessary to create this culture could by no means be guaranteed:

> Part of the barrier is about ensuring that those people actually involved start doing that thinking and it becomes part and parcel of how they think as managers. That potential's always there but the constraints are that your staff change all the time … There were constraints in that people have different views, that staff themselves, all of us, have all kinds of prejudices.
>
> (Equalities champion)

The GED and the use of EIAs were considered useful tools for assessing need across service providers, within increasingly complex arrangements for delivering services through commissioning and contracting. However they were also seen as a mixed blessing, with potential to catalyse a thoughtful approach but also to close it off and generate a reliance on mechanistic tick box processes. The challenge was to create thinking space to inform meaningful equalities work despite pressure to make quick decisions:

> You have to make sure that dialogue takes place all the time really.
>
> (Equalities champion)

The equalities champion saw herself as modelling 'tough love', a mixture of enabling a thoughtful approach to strategy and paying constant attention to the equalities agenda, modelling learning and sustaining dialogue:

> None of us have got the script completely right. We've got to challenge ourselves on a regular basis … that notion of questioning. The EIAs allow one to question. So suddenly in asking [what is] the nature of discrimination [that] might potentially be faced we realise there's a gap in the way we understood the analysis that's come off all the data.
>
> (Chair of CEB)

This case study is unique in claiming a history of consistent senior management and political leadership who saw equality and diversity as 'core business' and a valuable resource, not to be lost but to be embedded within modernisation. Modernisation was seen as an extension of previous politically driven and strand specific equalities agendas, unlike other case studies where it seemed to be positioned in opposition to a past that had to be left behind. There was a sense of security and stability, in contrast to our other case studies.

The overall narrative of senior managers was an optimistic, hopeful one of learning culture and incremental change. This was not unlike the vision from the corporate equalities team in Case Study 1. The challenges described were generic, relating to how to create a learning culture, and positioned as management and leadership driven. There was little specific reference to contested meanings of gender equality or of gender, and the overall discourse was one of discrimination and disadvantage, of 'addressing gaps' by identifying different gender needs and experiences in order to create equal opportunities within a level playing field.

In these accounts of a favourable political environment, legislation and the GED seemed to assume little importance as a support for embattled gender equality work. Rather, this local authority was confident in its capacity to sustain a strong commitment to equality despite changes in the national political environment. Indeed the legislation was considered to have the potential to undermine creative and independent thinking on equalities.

> Talking to my colleagues about how would we look at next year's service planning, how do you get that sort of thinking going? Having lots of duties and having a framework is supposed to be helpful and indeed I think in some situations it is, you know. It gives a kind of impetus, a kick to things. But you absolutely strangle people's real understanding of inequality and being able to do anything ... some have got great charts and you have to fill it in ... you know so it comes off as a mechanistic piece of paper that people have got to fill in and they'd done it, which you can do without thinking about any of it.
>
> (Equalities champion)

Our conversation had begun with an account that suggested that this local authority had arrived at a culture in which commitment to equality and diversity was unquestionably at its core. By the end of our conversation we had arrived at the nub of the issue: how do you 'get that sort of thinking going'? How do you move from a technocratic approach to compliance, to a thoughtful approach that enables people to develop 'real understanding' and practice that makes a difference to communities rather than only meeting government targets?

Case study 4: Promoting women's equality through collaborative feminist leadership

This case study organisation is a regional county administration, in contrast to the city authorities of the other case studies. The political administration changed during our research from Liberal Democrat to Conservative at which point our formal research access was withdrawn. We therefore had no access to senior managers in this local authority. Our data reflects the approach to equality of the previous regime as the impact of this change for the future was uncertain at the time of our research.

The county is characterised by diverse scattered communities built around market and coastal towns with a city as a regional centre. Overall quality of life is described as high, with pockets of disadvantage, where rural isolation and intolerance lead to prejudice and discrimination. The county council employed approximately 15,000 staff at the time or our visit, of which 7,000 worked in schools. Equalities leadership was located in a council equality strategy group made up of trade unions, a corporate equality officer located in Organisational Development, the directorate based equality and customer service champions, an elected member and officer 'champion' for equality and an independent reference group of experts for each equality strand who were contracted and paid for their involvement.

The council was working towards level 3 of the Equality Standard.[6] The equality policy and scheme refer to fairness and equal opportunity: eliminating discrimination and harassment, promoting equality of opportunity, promoting good relations and positive attitudes towards all people, and encouraging participation in public life. A programme of equalities work had been developed by the corporate equality advisor, and was designed to achieve compliance with legislation within service departments and external partnerships with service providers. A clear picture emerged from our interviews with her of the important contribution made by independent feminist organisations and experts in shaping this programme, interpreting the GED and its implementation. Despite the political instability within the authority, close-knit networks of equalities advisors, individual gender and women's equality consultants and activists emerged as key agents in supporting the development of strategy and collaborative learning within the region.

A regional strategic partnership made up of public, private, voluntary and community sector organisations worked together to 'deliver real improvements that matter to people of the region'. The equalities scheme was described as a 'living rather than a static document' and was based on consultation activities with each equality strand. A Gender Issues Group, reporting to the strategic partnership, had organised an open conference to identify priorities to be addressed by the GED. In relation to this point there is some similarity between this case study and Case Study 2.

We interviewed the corporate equality advisor and, at her invitation, a key gender equality activist from local and regional gender equality organisations. We then met with members of the independent feminist organisation that had been formed from and replaced the local authority gender equality forum, and a corporate equality advisor within the partnership organisation. The equalities advisor had a large budget at her disposal and stressed the importance of this in building community organisation and networks to generate an evidence base to support women's and gender equality work. She stressed the importance of external support networks and of collaborative leadership:

> The equality partnership is great, it's my baby I suppose and I am very proud of it. We all really enjoy coming together and having those meetings and those discussions and there are a lot of things that possibly wouldn't have happened without having that forum. ... We tend to talk about leadership as individuals and I think it's about collective leadership.
>
> (Corporate equality advisor)

A noticeable contrast emerged between the hopeful narrative of learning and incremental change, predominant in conversation with the corporate equalities officer when we met her at work, and the feminist narrative of struggle for transformational change that characterised discussions with the independent activists who were key players in influencing and shaping strategy. Only when we met off site, in discussion with her feminist ally, did the equality officer speak of the toll taken by conflict and embattlement that was, in her experience, an inevitable aspect of equality work and of the necessity for support networks to sustain her as a practitioner:

> I think the largest part of my support ... my support mechanisms which I need around me because otherwise I'd go mad, are outside the organisation, but I could count them on one hand ... I have to fight for stuff ... I am quite a challenging person and think the more challenging I am, the more I get side-lined.
>
> (Corporate equality advisor)

Towards the end of our discussion, a war metaphor shattered the hopeful narrative of incremental change that the equality officer had presented in an earlier interview:

> So I have to play my game very, very carefully and I am having to constantly ... it's like going to war, you are constantly having to re-strategise you know, what bomb do you use this week? ... Sometimes there are fights that are just not worth fighting, or I have to be devious.
>
> (Corporate equality advisor)

Although the GED was seen as an important mobilising tool, in the context of limited political commitment there were concerns about the quality of its implementation:

> One thing that bothers me about the mechanisms that we've got and I think the GED is really good because it's not reactive, its proactive, and ... but I still think it's possible to tick the boxes and write the strategies and actually not really have it touch the sides, not really have it make a difference, and

I think there's a huge amount of lip service and I don't necessarily think that's cynical, I think that people just do not get it and understand.

(Corporate equality advisor)

There was concern about the variable quality of mainstreaming equality in the context of loss of gender perspective and uncertain understanding of inequality as it specifically affected women. It was felt that a mainstreaming approach still required equalities experts with an understanding of gender inequality in order to build an evidence base to support the equality schemes required by the legislation:

> Well, it's the whole debate about mainstreaming isn't it? You know, you put [equality] into the mainstream, but you do need a specialist to feed the mainstream and provide the analysis. People thought they could do away with it if people got the hang of it but people don't because you have to think about it in a different kind of way.
>
> (Member of regional women's equality campaigning organisation)

There was a difference here between the feminist view of a 'different kind of a way' and the equality advisor's initial more hopeful account of how legal requirements had opened opportunities for incremental change, through learning and conversation. She referred to the difficulty of measuring impact, when your objective is to change people's thinking, and understandings, and when gender inequality as a concept was fast disappearing:

> It's very difficult when you are talking about equality to really measure the impact you are having on people ... It's not about, let's just be outcome focused, or let's be process focused, you need both. I don't think people have quite got that yet. You need the processes to get the outcomes.
>
> (Corporate equality advisor)

A lack of committed and knowledgeable leadership on equality was considered to be one of the main reasons that implementation of the GED was partial:

> There's a lot of box ticking stuff going on but there's little leadership and I think there's little leadership because there's a lack of analysis and understanding ... we need mechanisms that do not presume understanding but actually enable people to get to the core of things.
>
> (Corporate equality advisor)

Unlike our other case study authorities, senior women were not referred to as potential allies for a feminist change agenda, but sometimes as a barrier:

> There's a sense of creeping patriarchy and there's also a sense of women having crossed to the other side.
>
> (Member of regional women's equality campaigning organisation)

> There are women at the top who are quite frankly nasty ... they're not mentoring other women and helping them come through the ranks. They want to get into those positions of power and they do it by suppressing other women ... which is what you'd expect in an organisation that truly believes in gender equality and really wanted to do some maybe positive action with regards to women doesn't happen. Apparently the queen wasp emits a hormone, which completely renders all the other female wasps incapable of breeding or achieving. So she basically turns them into her slaves ... that exactly what's going on with these women ... queen wasps!
>
> (Corporate equality officer)

In contrast, the conference organised by the Gender Issues Group had raised a clear set of priorities to be addressed by the Strategic Partnership. Attended by a hundred women from a variety of community and regional organisations, the case was forcefully made for creation of a forum which would help women provide peer support, build consensus and inject women's ideas and energy into planning, delivery and scrutiny of services delivered by the county council. Following the conference, an independent regional feminist organisation had formed and replaced the Gender Issues Group that had been chaired by the local authority. This independent status was felt to be to be more effective as a lobby by both the equality advisor and members, who included trade unionists, Labour Party members and members of local voluntary organisations. Moreover, its affiliation to an established national feminist organisation provided both profile and access to research and an evidence base lost or missing from the local authorities. Members of this group saw themselves as challenging the quality of gender equality schemes and impact assessments required by the GED, and ensuring that priorities identified in local consultation with women were reflected in the various annual planning and resource documents for the local authority and the inter-agency partnerships of public service providers. In order to do this they stressed the important strategic role of independent feminist voice and organisation:

> A couple of us said that focusing on quality was not the same as focusing on equality, like there is a huge difference ... the people in the council found that quite uncomfortable ... so it did get kind of hairy because we were being quite challenging I think ... But now we say things like ... we are challenging and we are here to challenge you and you really need to hear this. So we're developing a kind of agreement, I think, within the larger group.
>
> (Member of regional women's equality campaigning organisation)

The case study illustrates how the GED provided, in the absence of consistent political and senior management commitment to equality, a vital instrument for the equality advisor to put together a gender equality scheme that was grounded in community consultation, offering opportunities for collaborative leadership.

The GED was also the primary instrument used by independent feminist organisations to hold the local authority to account, and to challenge their interpretation of gender equality. The collaborative leadership exercised between independent advocacy groups, trade unions and the equality advisor enabled feminist content to be brought to performance targets and plans. Alongside the GED, the Equality Standard and Equality Framework were used to build an evidence base that mapped onto the local authorities' performance measures, on which resource allocation was based.

In summary, this case study was distinctive geographically and in its status as a rural county authority. There was reference in discussion with participants and in documentation to pockets of discrimination and to demographic change. The equality discourse was one of fairness: challenging inequality and celebrating diversity. The structures developed for equality work were networked and the focus was on partnership working with service providers and experts from independent and local community organisations. There was no equality team here, but a single corporate equality advisor who supported departmental staff with an equalities advisory brief which they held alongside their day jobs. She used her budget to promote external equality networks and to sustain strong links with local feminist organisations to sustain her work and push the boundaries of what could be addressed. Since then, however, the regional equality network has lost its funding.

The case for strong autonomous feminist organisation was made by the local group who broke away from the local authority. The group was led by feminist activists with experience of leadership in trade union and political parties. This experience and knowledge of how decision making within the local authority worked, enabled them to engage with and to shape processes for implementing the GED within the council. They were able to draw from their knowledge of diversity within local communities to effectively challenge the authority's interpretation of gender impact and to engage with intersectionality from a feminist perspective. Interestingly, in contrast to an earlier focus on independent feminist action, on our follow-up research visit we were told by one of the activists that her frustration at a lack of feminist leadership within the local authority had led her to stand for and win election as a councillor. In essence a strategy of 'in and against the state' had emerged (see Chapters 3 and 4).

Case study 5: Balancing intersectionality, 'cohesion' and cuts

Our final case study is a city that describes itself as the largest centre of culture, employment and education in its region. It has historically been a commercial port and in more recent years the economy has depended on the creative media, electronics and aerospace industries, and the city centre docks have been regenerated as a centre of heritage and culture. The population is diverse, 16 per cent black and ethnic minority and, in common with other case studies, increasing in diversity in younger generations. There was a recent history of tension and civil unrest in ethnic minority communities in the authority. At the time of our research the council was the largest employer in the city, employing around

17,000 staff, 40 per cent of which worked in schools. The political administration of the city had until recently been Labour, and more recently Liberal Democrat, in coalition with Labour and the Green Party.

There is a strong history and culture of independent political activism, including feminism, from the nineteenth century. A political approach to equality and diversity is still reflected in the authority's equality and diversity policy documents, where, in contrast to Case Studies 1 and 2, there are references to recognition of oppression, disadvantage and multiple discrimination. There is a stated commitment to putting right inequality through positive action with recognition that varied backgrounds are an asset to the city.

It is therefore rather surprising that the corporate equality and cohesion team was small in comparison with other urban authorities, and cohesion had recently been included in its remit. However, in contrast to other case studies, there was a generic equality post and two departmental posts with specific remits for gender, a women's forum made up of women's organisations in the city, and a women's network for employees. There were extensive training programmes on diversity and equality for all staff and positive action to encourage more women into senior positions. A strategic corporate equality working group chaired by an executive director, a committed feminist, reported to the corporate board of executive directors. This had recently replaced a less senior equality forum that was considered to be ineffective, a change recommended by a review carried out as part of the bid to reach level 4 of the Equality Standard. All departments had gender equality action plans in place. These extensive equality policies and practices were seen as exemplary in the region, and the equalities team were looked to for support by smaller rural authorities in the region. The local authority had achieved level 3 of the Equality Standard and was preparing to apply for level 4.

In our two visits to this local authority we interviewed the Chief Executive, the elected politician with responsibility for leading on social cohesion, equality and diversity, senior managers who chaired the corporate equalities working group, corporate and departmental equality team members, the divisional director of Human Resources, and members of a local women's organisation. Despite an outward appearance of established equality practice, we again found a local authority in flux, with a history of political instability and of ever-changing coalitions in which equality slipped up and down the list of priorities. The corporate equality team seemed to mirror this instability, with the gender equality officer frequently seconded to a service department leading to a sense of fragmentation and lack of continuity in her work.

Between our two visits there was another change in political administration and in corporate leadership introducing major restructuring, with a stated intention of introducing a more outcome focused business based approach to equality. Change fatigue was reflected in the tone of discussions with our interviewees, some of whom were invested in embracing 'smarter targets' for equality work, while others conveyed a sense of frustration at the gap between gender equality policy and management practice.

It's intangible almost. It would be hard to sort of say in any definite ... you couldn't write a manual about it. But it is, sometimes it's like slogging through treacle, because it is, it's just going back, back and back.

(Gender equality advisor)

There was a sense of dependence on external levers and experts, strongly motivated external groups, and committed female senior managers to achieve outcomes. The Equality Standard had proved to be one such useful lever to achieve stronger senior commitment to achieving results, but there was some hesitation about how far this led to actual outcomes:

I think Standards are a really interesting one, because I think they are interesting in helping us focus on the kind of things we should be doing. Whether they really help us deliver the outcome, I'm never entirely sure.

(Gender equality advisor)

We were told consistently that the local authority was 'superb on processes, poor on outcomes' and creating processes to address this seemed to be a focus of the current restructure. The corporate equalities team was developing 'smarter targets' with departments for their service plans, with input from stakeholder groups. The challenge was to identify measures that would relate to outcomes, as anything that could not be measured was deemed not to count, in the 'business transformation' agenda. The equalities team referred to their wish for a stronger challenge from stakeholder groups, to compensate for a policy process that was fallible and largely consisted of a jumble of targets with insufficient ownership.

The GED had been the driver for a gender equality action plan and scheme to be drawn up, on the basis of data collected through a city-wide consultation exercise with women who had been commissioned some time previously, by the leader of the council (see Chapter 4). Despite this, there was a sense of lack of ownership of the gender agenda and concern that if stakeholders did not engage there was no problem to solve.

Legislation does not require the use of research, only consultation with stakeholders. However, there is a sense that, unless stakeholders say that there is disadvantage, there is no case to be made.

(Equality advisor, legal services)

There were some strong and effective external lobbies that had achieved results on specific gender and equality issues in resourcing specific services, particularly in relation to domestic violence. The external lobbies were supported by committed individual senior managers, but this seemed precarious and was not equivalent to an overall strategy. Interestingly, the fact that a woman led the local authority seemed to encourage belief that gender was no longer an issue. An equalities advisor stated that 'there was a mistaken perception that things have shifted more than they actually have, with increased numbers of senior women'.

This was the only local authority where we had access to interviews with the Chief Executive, a woman, and the lead politician holding the equality and diversity brief. Our discussions with them were more reflective in tone and less solution focused than many others. This was useful in providing space for challenges to be named and complexity explored without pressure to demonstrate that solutions could easily be found. For the purposes of this case study we will focus on two of the distinctive themes that surfaced in these interviews: the difficulty of getting the structures right to support equality within complex commissioning processes introduced by outsourcing of local authority services; and how to address intersectional issues within equality impact assessments.

The financial challenges of looking at equalities were raised right at the beginning of our discussion with the Chief Executive. These she defined as a 'tricky balance' between downsizing and trying to get a workforce profile that was more reflective of the community the authority served.

> The only way we can downsize without making a massive redundancy bill is actually to retrain and recycle the people we have got. ... If we continue to do that then we don't necessarily change the profile.
>
> (Chief Executive)

The move from being direct providers to commissioning of public services required change in how equality was to be built into commissioning processes. The Chief Executive felt that the City Council had not yet achieved appropriate processes, particularly for engaging citizens. The move to joint commissioning by partnerships of public service organisations introduced a further layer of complexity as a shared equality framework would need to be developed that could build equality outcomes into the specifications:

> We are not yet at the point of having a robust commissioning service ... so there's a question of how you engage service users in that so that you can then reflect on what's being delivered. ... We have got a lot more work to do first to get a common commissioning framework that we can use council wide that is fit for purpose and we are not there yet. ... How to do that in a partnership way and at the same time to recognise that there are quite rightly the need for different processes, depending on the size of the package and the outcomes ... What should the model look like that will allow us to deliver those outcomes and engage people in services and how we scope them and at what point in which parts of the process do we bring those things in? What's your check and balance? It's about how you have expert advice liaising with frontline service and delivery to pull together a mechanism where you can actually procure or commission. ... The question I always ask is getting the right people at the right points in the process to make sure you have the right impact.
>
> (Chief Executive)

The discussion demonstrated the strategic challenges for the organisation of equality work posed by the replacement of direct provision by commissioning of public services by the local authority and within inter-organisational partnerships. The role of independent advocacy in this process was important, as was liaising with the voluntary and third sectors. This was not straightforward either, as advocacy might conflict with their role as potential contractors.

In our discussion with the elected member of the council who held the brief for equality, diversity and social cohesion, the multi-ethnic nature of the city's population and the diversity of public service delivery required to meet different needs was an area of pressing concern. The history of racial unrest in the city had almost certainly increased the focus on issues of social cohesion in this case study. In a city with very wealthy, largely white, suburbs and poor, urban white and ethnic minority enclaves, social cohesion was always going to be a difficult project.

The councillor illustrated how tick box approaches to equality could overlook issues of social cohesion, with, as an example, a decision to house Somali families in a locality where there had been racist attacks:

> Can you see, people hadn't worked this out. They'd done an equalities impact assessment around race and there was just a sentence in there about BME households. They hadn't actually thought about what the community cohesion impact would be. They'd done the race bit on an EIA and said, potentially this will benefit BME families ... but they hadn't thought about the community cohesion issues in the community. How are we going to cope with this? What are we going to do? Do we actually have to vary the allocation policy? ... They'd done what I would call the mechanical equality diversity bit, but they hadn't done ... you know, I said to them cohesion is more than equality and diversity. I don't want to call it a tick box exercise, but they hadn't widened it out to a community cohesion agenda.
>
> (Lead politician, cohesion, equality and diversity)

The councillor went on to explore a number of challenges posed by lack of awareness of how the local authority might be reproducing class and race stereotypes in its publicity materials, and how this had been successfully challenged when brought to the attention of the equalities officers. His example of problematic publicity to attract young people to the city illustrated the uncertainty of how gender equality is understood and what images might promote it:

> It had a crowd of young people drinking champagne on a terrace. Given the diversity of the city, there wasn't a single non-white face in the picture shot. ... It wasn't about gender because there were men and women.
>
> (Lead politician, cohesion, equality and diversity)

During the interview we explored the crossover between different equality strands and the difficulty of addressing intersectional issues, in particular clashes between faith, and gender and sexual orientation. Here the emphasis was simultaneously on the difficulty of working across all of the strands and the determination to do so:

> It's not a pick and mix exercise when you look at equality strands as far as I am concerned. There might be something in what we do that, particularly the faith community, might have some difficulty with. We are prepared to work flexibly etc. but we're not going to step away from those duties we've got. We've got an issue around belief and LGB issues which have come to the fore in schools, which is actually portrayed as a Muslim issue. It's not; it's a Christian issue as well … You can't shy away, but it's actually a question about engagement of dialogue around these issues and preventative work.
>
> (Lead politician, cohesion, equality and diversity)

The focus on social cohesion tended to rather swamp gender as a separate equality strand. Reference was made by the councillor to work with Muslim women's organisations as community cohesion, defined as helping people get along together. He considered cohesion to be the approach adopted in the local authority, which he contrasted to the government prevention of extremism agenda.

Our findings shared many of the features of the previous case studies: an anticipated relocation of the corporate equality team in the context of organisational restructuring, efficiency savings and frequent references to individual female managers who were relied upon to prioritise gender equality issues. The corporate equality, diversity and cohesion team was located in the community development function, and this was reflected in what appeared to be the close working relationships with community and voluntary organisations within specific equality strands, including a local branch of the national Fawcett Society. The two interviews with the Chief Executive and the lead politician for equality, diversity and cohesion and others conducted for our research within this local authority, highlighted the contested meanings of equality in relation to all of the specific strands. The history of racial tension in this case study meant that social cohesion was at the forefront of the equalities agenda. The move towards joint multi-agency commissioning where each organisation brought its own understanding of equality and implementation practices highlighted the need for joint frameworks for equality to be developed. Alongside this there were the challenges of engaging with equality across separately organised strands, where strategies to meet intersecting needs triggered clashes of belief between communities. While there was commitment to addressing intersectionality, in practice it seemed that the need to do so arose only where there was a conflict of interests. Gender and women's equality did not seem to be a priority, other than in specific areas, one of which was violence. Once more the equalities team seemed to lead a precarious existence and emphasised their dependence on external groups to assert a women's equality gender perspective challenge within consultation exercises and scrutiny processes. The result was to create an imbalance between competing equality lobbies, reliant on individual experience for their effectiveness.

The Gender Equality Duty: an effective instrument for sustaining the long agenda for women's and gender equality?

The GED introduced the kind of legislation that many advocates of gender equality in local government had been waiting for – a shift from a negative duty to eliminate sex discrimination to a positive duty for public authorities to promote gender equality (Chapter 3). In all of our case study organisations we found a proactive approach to promoting equality and not merely a focus on removing discrimination. This was made explicit in policy documents and tool kits for implementation, where there was emphasis on the positive case for promoting women into leadership alongside measures to combat specific areas of discrimination and disadvantage such as sexual violence and unequal pay. The legal duty to promote equality and good relations as well as to eliminate discrimination lent legitimacy to the proactive approach already taken by equalities teams and committed managers and politicians in each of our case study organisations. Nevertheless, there was precariousness in the gender equality project itself. There were repeated references to a loss of gender sensibility and to the loss of women employees as an organised force for change within local authorities. The organisation of equality work as a generic, undifferentiated concept was driven by a government agenda posited as 'business transformation', which had lost its roots in outward facing participative democracy, and democratically accountable local services.

Leadership and expertise for women's and gender equality work was formally located in corporate teams and champions within the new business and performance structures and processes. However, the business case for specialist equalities teams was being eroded in the reorganisations taking place. In one of our case studies, equality teams had been replaced by business planning partners and generic equality champions. In this context, expertise held within stakeholder networks was assuming a greater significance. In Case Studies 2 and 3, specific expertise in women's equality was held within networks of committed individuals, organised within the local authority and externally. Within these networks knowledge was exchanged, strategies developed and women's equality work sustained in increasingly adverse circumstances. Links with national policy networks and campaigns were important, enabling access to feminist perspectives, and an extensive up to date knowledge base and strategy.

The rationale for promoting equality needed to be based on a business case that demonstrated value for 'customers' in local communities. In local authorities under extreme budgetary pressure, making a business case for equality was often a difficult project, perhaps best illustrated by the very tense and protracted equal pay settlements undertaken in most local authorities, including our case studies. Equality advisors spoke of the need to translate 'equality' into the more acceptable discourse of 'quality' in order to protect and embed it in mainstream performance led processes. While this had the desired effect of removing dysfunctional conflict associated with the past, it cut the transformative roots from the gender equality project, relocating this wider agenda with external campaigns and stakeholders.

A key challenge in each of our case study organisations was the predominance of liberal level playing field notions of gender equality, and the belief that women's equality had been achieved and was, therefore, no longer a legitimate priority or sustainable as an agenda in its own right. A number of factors had contributed to this perception, not least the loss of a Left Labour movement with a vision of extended local democracy, the loss of an independent feminist movement engaging with local authorities with a vision of the long agenda for transformation of gender relations throughout society and the general lack of critical gender awareness as a frame of reference within local authorities. Changes in political leadership, as in Case Studies 2, 4 and 5, where newly elected administrations had replaced strategy seeking to address systemic inequality with equal opportunities for individuals, were also strong contributing factors.

The GED required public bodies to put together a gender equality scheme (GES) based on stakeholder consultation, and to make this publically available. All our case study organisations had done this and were currently updating and reviewing their plans. Yet, where there were no independent women's organisations, there was widespread confusion about how to consult on gender equality. There was often an assumption that if women and men were both present in consultation events then the job had been done. In other words, women and men's physical presence at mixed gender events was conflated with capacity to address gender specific priorities and concerns. In Case Studies 2, 3, 4 and 5 'gender' was interpreted by feminists as 'women' and by others as an invitation to make a case for men to be given equivalent resources, for example, for sheltered accommodation for men fleeing domestic violence. Nevertheless, the requirement to base gender equality schemes on stakeholder consultation did provide opportunities for independent women's organisations to assert their priorities and to influence generic strategy and business planning processes. In each of the case studies independent feminist networks played a vital role in keeping gender equality on the agenda, and injecting critical engagement with the predominant liberal discourses of gender equality within the local authority. Local feminist organisations were particularly effective where linked to national policy networks and campaigns, as in Case Studies 1, 2, 4 and 5. It was as if radical discourses of women's and gender equality had been outsourced, brought in via expert consultants to assist with compliance, voiced through requirements to consult with independent organisations or discussed within equalities practitioner networks.

In each of our case studies an increasingly diverse population was an issue for public service provision. While they all embraced the single equality duty as a way of dealing more successfully with intersectional equality issues, most also emphasised the importance of maintaining strand specific schemes. While the positive duties at the time of the research were limited to race, gender and disability, additional regulations required elimination of discrimination on grounds of age, religion and belief, sexual orientation and transgender. All case study organisations had policies in place that anticipated extension to these groups within a single positive equality duty. Some of them expressed concern at the difficulty of sustaining a women's equality agenda once the GED was replaced by a generic equality duty. Their strategy was to 'future proof' against legislative change by embedding gender equality into business planning processes, and to build an evidence base that could be used in the years ahead. The GED, while it existed, protected the work that had been done, as well as legitimating proactive strategies for promoting gender equality as one strand in a generic equality duty.

In each of our case studies, equality impact assessments (EIAs) were a key instrument for implementing the GED, but posed a number of challenges. One of these challenges was the diffused accountability introduced by the outsourcing and procurement of public services, and the complexity of multi-agency partnerships for commissioning and delivering services, led by local authorities. In one of our case studies, a common framework for conducting EIAs had been negotiated and was an important instrument for developing common strategy for equality across partner organisations. Building capacity to conduct EIAs effectively and consistently within and across these different organisation cultures and systems was a challenge that had yet to be met; building internal capacity was a priority and a focus for discussion in our interviews with all the equalities teams. In Case Studies 1, 2 and 3 this was described as an incremental process from which contestation associated with previous politically driven agendas had been removed. Within this narrative, gender equality was constructed as politically neutral, consistent with quality, good public service ethos and customer service. Gendered power had been removed from the equation and equality was often measured in statistical terms.[7] In all of the case studies the evidence base to make a case for change was constructed in quantitative terms, demonstrating disadvantage or 'gaps' for members of equality strands and measured against performance targets. There was no language for unmasking the workings of gender inequality in the distribution of resources and governance, for addressing intersectionality or the systemic roots of inequality. The equality practitioners in our case studies worked hard to improve the quality of EIAs but the incorporation of such an important aspect of the GED into a business led agenda had resulted in frustration amongst feminist activists, and the labelling of EIAs as 'tick box exercises'. This is a discourse that has since been exploited by leading national politicians in the attempt to discredit and dismantle the subsequent public sector equality duty.

To conclude, the GED provided an essential framework for sustaining and protecting commitment to women's equality in the context of reorganisations based on business planning and outsourced services. The requirement to consult, and to conduct EIAs, opened up opportunities to develop structures and processes to hold service directors to account, and to build an evidence base to make the case for equality initiatives in the future within specific service areas. Our case studies provide the evidence that while the GED played a vital role in promoting the mainstreaming of gender equality work, through a positive duty of compliance, it was not sufficient to guarantee outcomes, or avoidance of a technocratic tick box approach. How the opportunities provided by the legal duties were taken up within local authorities was reliant upon knowledge and understanding of gendered power and its intersections with other forms of inequality, individual commitment to act on this knowledge, and the existence of collective organisation to promote gender equality. The willingness to enact the legislation came from committed individuals who were women and men (but mostly women) who held roles as managers, equalities advisors, trade unionists and political leaders. Progress came when they were willing and able to engage with challenges from independent organisations and were prepared to use the legislation to call colleagues within their local authorities to account.

On re-reading the interview transcripts at the time of writing we were struck by the enormity of the gender equality change project and the complexity of the practices and skills required in achieving it. The contributors to our research were architects of mechanisms for gender and equality mainstreaming and facilitators of a perceptual shift towards ownership of a case for gender equality and its intersections with other equality strands. The systems they described were extraordinarily complex, involving adoption of standards and targets across internal and external multi-agency partnerships for procurement, commissioning and contracting. They were helped by legislation, national benchmarks and audit, but relied on committed managers and politicians to facilitate the thoughtful engagement and dialogue with stakeholders needed to enact these in a meaningful way. So, in addition to being architects of systems for compliance and assessment, they were coaches and mentors, facilitators of learning, interpreters and translators, who reframed the gender equality project into a language that was recognisable and acceptable to a shifting, sometimes hostile, political leadership (Page, 2011). Invariably this meant adopting a politically neutral discourse of quality and fairness requiring patience, resilience and sophisticated relational skills. As co-researchers we found ourselves in strong debates about what the disappearing of women's inequality meant. It was clear that there was a wish to avoid the conflict associated with earlier conceptualisations of municipal feminism, and that the discourse of incremental change had replaced it. Yet it was also evident that this was a view held more strongly by those at the corporate centre, while others who were closer to the interface with service managers, trade union representatives or independent feminist organisations, referred more frequently to compliance and 'iron fist in velvet glove'. Was the discourse of incremental change a sign of selling out, evidence of a lost agenda, or of effective gender mainstreaming? Had women's equality taken a step forward or a step back? In the light of our research findings and what has happened to the equality legislation and women's equality more generally since, we take up these questions and debates in Chapter 6.

Notes

1 The research reported on in this chapter consists of a pilot study in five case study local authorities funded by the British Academy.
2 In 2006 results only three local authorities in the country had achieved levels 4 and 5, in contrast to 60 at level 3, 129 at level 2 and 162 at level 1.
3 Young adults Not in Employment, Education or Training.
4 See Chapter 3, n.4.
5 This continues to be a widespread assumption within local authorities, arising from a Best Value performance indicator requiring local authorities to report annually on the percentage of women employees in their top 5 per cent of earners. Monitored by the Audit Commission, local authorities were graded according to their performance and progress.
6 In 2006, of all county councils, only 10 had achieved level 1, 15 at level 2, eight at level 3 and none at levels 4 and 5. This shows lower levels of achievement to metropolitan and urban city councils.
7 The Equalities Measurement Framework, drawn up by the EHRC.

6 Chasing the dream

Feminists and researchers creating spaces for change

The opening page of this book contains a quote from an equalities advisor in one of our case study authorities:

> The whole [of] equalities work is like that really. Running around with a butterfly net!

She was referring to the beautiful but ephemeral nature of the vision of equality and the inadequacy of the tools to capture it, the difficulty in arriving at an end point, and perhaps the impossibility of it ever being a completed project. Although the metaphor of chasing after an elusive dream does convey something of the essential nature of gender equality work, in common with all social justice aspirations, gender equality is best described as a direction of travel, a project in which participants are invited to play an active part rather than a single destination.

The capacity for 'optimistic imagining' was characteristic among reformers and radicals in America and Britain during the late nineteenth and early twentieth centuries (Rowbotham, 2010, p.1):

> From the 1880s, thought interacted with action in a whirl of speculation, proposals, policies and utopian visions. Exploratory and adventurous aspirations were expressed not only in books and articles, but through movements, organisations, local groups and projects. Women, along with men, were swept up in the impetus of changing everyday life.

Many of the debates of that earlier period are surprisingly reminiscent of issues still pursued by feminists today. The Women's Liberation Movement (WLM) of the 1970s inspired and was inspired by similar dreams of transforming social relations both within domestic relations and in relation to the state (Rowbotham, 1990). In both periods campaigns directed at the state ran alongside experiments to alter daily life and culture. Dreams of women's equality evolved and were lived out in social relations in domestic, social, political and economic spheres, and were expressed in poetry, drama and a wide variety of cultural forms. Within the spaces that opened up, discontent, aspirations and desires were shared, and contested. There was passion, and exhilaration, as different experiences of oppression were voiced and shared.

The history of the struggle for women's and gender equality within the local state that we examined in Chapters 3, 4 and 5 is but one facet of attempts to translate these dreams into lived reality. As we saw in Chapter 5 attempts to translate a vision of social change into an institutional form that can survive in inhospitable political contexts runs the risk of closing down a dynamic, trans-formational, creative process into a set of static prescriptive regulations. There is a need to hold the tension between policies that establish what is possible in the here and now, *and* a live dialogic process of inquiry and of imagining what might be the desired goal.

In the rest of this chapter we take up the idea of dreams and imagination as being at the centre of radical transformational change in relation to feminist practice in the local state, past and future. We consider some of the potential roles for researchers in supporting creative and generative forms of knowledge production, critically engaging with the assumptions that inform the change practice of key actors and organisations identified within our research.

Can utopian thinking be a resource for sustaining feminist transformational practice within the local state?

Utopian thinking is often seen as a way of disengaging from the practice of social change. Alternatively, it can offer a method and a way of finding form for imagined alternatives (Levitas, 2013). Desire and longing for what is not experienced has catalysed utopian imagination and hope in feminist movements. It challenges what has previously been taken for granted alongside the belief that another world is possible. Utopian thinking is the precursor to pre-figurative practice and activism (Rowbotham, 2010).

Both utopian thinking and prefigurative social action are inspired by a deep sense that something is missing; a lack that cannot be articulated other than by imagining its fulfilment. Levitas (2013) makes a distinction between utopian visions that offer, or are interpreted as, a blueprint of a future desired state and utopian visions that offer an invitation to imagine a future. In the latter case, there is no prescription for how society ought to be, but rather an opening of space for invention and imagination as a way of generating new knowledge. Following Bloch (1986), Levitas posits the existence of a utopian impulse as a form of anticipatory consciousness, a form of 'forward dreaming' that is a necessary element in the production of the future (Bloch, 1986, cited in Levitas, 2013, p.6). Utopian imagination is fragmentary, ephemeral and can be glimpsed in myth, fairy tale, music, poetry philosophy and the arts, as well as political activity and experimentation in ways of living. On this basis, Levitas makes a case for utopian thinking as a method for the imaginary reconstitution of society:

> Utopian thinking is in this case not about devising and imposing a blueprint. Rather it entails holistic thinking about the connections between economic,

social, existential and ecological processes in an integrated way. We can then develop alternative possible scenarios for the future and open these up to public debate and democratic decision – insisting always on the provisionality, reflexivity and contingency of what we are able to imagine, and in full awareness that utopian speculation is formed in the double squeeze of what we are able to imagine and what we are able to imagine as possible.

(Levitas, 2013, p.19)

In her study of the history of women's utopian writing, Bammer (1991) argues that 1970s feminists developed and expanded the genre of utopian writing and the idea of utopia. Moreover, that the feminisms of the 1970s recuperated the concept of utopia as a vital dimension of radical politics. For Bammer feminism itself is necessarily utopian, driven by anticipation, by the recognition that patriarchy is an unnatural state, and by the belief in and pursuit of an alternative. Both Bammer and Levitas define utopia as a journey, not a goal, demanding an open and indeterminate future. Both distinguish utopias that focused on the structures and organisation of an imagined new society from feminist utopian writing of the 1970s where the focus is on agency rather than structure. They make the case for holding the aesthetic and existential alongside the political and the social in our imagining of a better society and potential for flourishing (Bammer, 1991, p.19).

Other feminist writers locate themselves firmly in the socialist feminist tradition in which capitalism, shaped by and experienced through male-dominated economic and political power structures, is considered to remain the primary barrier to women's equality. In their recently updated volume of *Beyond the Fragments* (BTF) Rowbotham, Wainwright and Segal (2013) reflect on socialist feminist activism between the 1970s and the present. Here structure and agency are considered to be closely tied. As Rowbotham (2013, p.11) argues:

I could see the obvious snags of living utopia in the bad old world of capitalism, yet I was sure that the manner in which you organized affected the new society which you could bring about.

Wainwright (2013) highlights four threads that have a good deal of resonance with the themes of this book. The first of these threads is 'how far state institutions can be transformed in response to democratic pressures, rather than being submissive to the financial markets and big business' (p.37). The second thread 'concerns the political significance of how knowledge is understood and organised' (p.38). More specifically this thread is concerned with multiple ways of knowing and links to a third thread, the need for a plurality of ideas if coalitions of different interest groups are to be successfully mobilised in pursuit of a better future. The fourth thread brings us back to the state and how its position as either 'obstacle' or 'resource' will inevitably shape the way feminists organise (p.38).

What is clear from this writing is that the (liberating) state is crucial to bringing about women's equality, but its capture or 'opening up' depends on coalitions of activism that can see difference as a strength rather than a problem. The following section considers these arguments in terms of different utopias and the possibilities for coalition.

Beyond single utopias: intersectionality, divisions, dialogue and coalition

Competing utopias continue to impassion debate about the good society. *Occupy*, the *Arab Spring*, the *Indignados*, are all fuelled by visions of fairer and more equal societies, hope and belief that a better world is possible. But it would be a mistake to associate utopia only with redistributive visions and values. Notions of the global village, neo-liberal meritocracy, religious fundamentalisms, libertarianism, communitarianism, anarchism, communism and socialisms all hold at their core different and often deeply incompatible visions of the good society. Despite this, a repeated theme throughout the book is that coalitions that can unite across class, ethnicity, sexuality, disability and gender divides are required if transformational change is to be achieved.

Feminists have dreamed and imagined a variety of forms of gender equality within these different social relations. Many of their utopian texts and political visions reflect the cultural prejudices and limitations of the dreamers (Bammer, 1991) and describe an idealised future state. Based on similarity rather than difference, these imaginary worlds have often reproduced race and class divisions. Within the WLM in Great Britain, self-organisation based on discovery of a common cause that is limited to shared experience, and later shared identity, have often led to destructive exclusions and damaging disputes (Lovenduski and Randall, 1993). As we highlighted in Chapter 2 the history of black feminist organisation in the USA in the 1970s demonstrates a well-established history of addressing racial, sexual, heterosexual and class as interlocking systems of oppression (Combahee River Collective, 1983; Thornton Dill and Zambrana, 2009; Thompson, 2002). The distinction between the need for organisation based on communality, shared experience and identity and the need to make alliances across differences in order to arrive at common goals for women's equality was first made by black feminist writers and activists (Smith, 1983). In 1981, for example, Johnson Reagon (1983) called for alliances based on recognition of difference between women, and distinguished this from the need for and enjoyment of community based on affinity. In their key text *Bridges of Power*, Albrecht and Brewer (1990) wrote specifically of practices developed by US feminists to address divisions between women and to support their alliance building across differences of identity such as sexuality, ethnicity, race and class in local and transnational contexts. bell hooks (1981, 1991) powerfully challenges white feminists to acknowledge their racial and class privilege and to enter into dialogue with black feminists, breaking their collusion with racist stereotypes:

> This is an intervention. A message from that space in the margin that is a site of creativity and power, that inclusive space where we recover

ourselves, where we move in solidarity to erase the category colonized/
colonizer. Marginality as a site of resistance. Enter that space. Let us meet
there. Enter that space, we greet you as liberators.

(1991, p.152)

In the UK there is a history of calls for solidarity and alliance building
between women based on the one hand on recognition of differences of power
relating to class, race, disability and sexuality, and on the other hand rejection
of identity categories imposed by the state (see, for example, Mama, 1984;
Morris, 1993; Patel, 1999; Lind, 2004; Shapiro, 1996; Hick, 2000, 2005). Black
feminist activists have consistently and powerfully challenged white feminists'
view of black women, called for solidarity in their struggles against racialised
gender stereotypes within public services, welfare, immigration and employment legislation (see, for example, Lewis, 2002; Mulholland and Patel, 1999;
Wilson, 1978). A common thread in these accounts of activism in relation to the
local state is a concern to develop practices that engage with the intersections of
inequality, are robust enough to withstand the pressures of competition for
resources and political influence, and that support dialogue across political
divisions and communities of interest. In our research, however, we found little
evidence that this rich tradition of practice was available as a resource to
equality practitioners within the local state in the later periods (Chapter 5).
In contrast, in the earlier periods of municipal feminism, where activist and
equality practitioners were more closely linked, accommodating difference was
a key focus of the gender equality practice and, ironically, the aspect that was
most vilified in the press and by other dissenters. A useful role for researchers is
to make this tradition of practice and the problems that are likely to be
encountered in its implementation available to equality activist networks
orientated to the local state, and through participative research initiatives, to
offer spaces for their development.

In her research with feminist peace activists in three different war zones,
Cockburn (1998, 1999), takes up the term 'transversal politics' to analyse the
practices they developed for bridging differences across ethnic, political and
religious divides. First utilised by Italian feminist peace activists, and developed by
Yuval Davies (1997) the concept offers strategies for engaging with the contradiction posed by the dangers of the belief in universal sisterhood, and a relativist
stress on difference that threatens division and fragmentation (Cockburn, 1998,
p.8). While transversal politics is based on standpoint epistemology, it recog-
nises that knowledge based on just one positioning is 'unfinished'; dialogue is
the practice for arriving at a more complete understanding of how differences
are enmeshed with social, economic and political inequality in any specific
context (Yuval Davies, 1997, p.95).

In transversal politics perceived unity and homogeneity are replaced by
dialogues which give recognition to the specific positioning of those who
participate in them as well as to the 'unfinished knowledge' that each such

situated positioning can offer … The boundaries of transversal dialogue are determined by the message rather than by the messenger.

(Yuval Davies 1997, pp.130–31, cited in Cockburn, 1998, p.9)

This strategy has been developed by women activists as a way of bridging political divisions between feminists in international and local contexts. In a dialogue with Cynthia Cockburn, Pragna Patel (1999) draws from the practice and politics developed by Southall Black Sisters (SBS),[1] a collective of South Asian and African-Caribbean women in London, England and teases out what transversal politics offers to the practice of alliance and coalition building in relation to the local state. She begins by stating (p.117) that identity and alliance building are closely connected and that the history of SBS can be seen as a history of resisting imposed identities by the community, the anti-racist movement and the state:

> It's very easy to do what the state does, which is to elevate your experience somehow so that you see yourself as the only group that suffers. It puts you into competition with each other, and allows the state to demonise others, to exclude others.

(Patel, 1999, p.130)

In contrast to the organisation of equality work in local authorities into separate strands and categories, Patel states that the experience of black and minority ethnic women shows that the constructions of identity are constantly in a state of flux: 'They are forever being negotiated and renegotiated in social and political processes, here and abroad' (p.130). Patel argues that SBS aims to provide a secular space where dialogue can take place as a basis for alliance building. Transversal politics offers a strategy for enabling these alliances to go beyond service provision to building social movements, 'in order to bring about some kind of wider social transformation' (p.134).

   These accounts of strategy and practice for bridging difference in order to work towards a wider, transformational agenda for social change draw attention to the specificity of women's experiences and complex intersections between inequalities (Hill Collins, 1990). They offer a resource and potential for developing practices to address intersectionality within the current context of equality practice within the local state in Great Britain, where single equality duties have been replaced by the generic duty. The vision that underpins these accounts is one in which women support and engage with each other in a dialogue to construct a new and more equal society, a vision compatible with utopia as an unfinished project, a direction of travel, grounded in an understanding of the dynamics of unequal power and political change.

Building utopia in the local state

Feminist engagement with the local state in the 1980s and early 1990s was embedded in a normative vision of the local state of a particular kind: an agent of redistributive justice, an extended vision of inclusive democracy, a regulator of the market and of social relations. Femocracy, equal opportunities, managing diversity and gender mainstreaming were subsequently introduced as gendered strategies embedded within a vision of social democracy. Women from diverse communities were to participate equally in governance, employment and leadership and to benefit equally as citizens and service users through redirection of funding and resources.

As we have seen in Chapters 3 and 4, there is evidence that fragments of this utopian vision in the gender and women's equality practices developed. These fragments serve as potent reminders that in moments it has been possible to creatively engage with intersectional interests in local and international contexts. The memory of the NGO Forum in Beijing, for example, and the collective work to make visible, to enable participation and to develop services by engaging with different communities of women in local authorities, continue to ignite hope and desire for change. Participation in these events has produced powerful collective memories, embodied in lived experience, that have inspired protocols and policy as well as structures and processes to support promotion of gender equality. However our research demonstrates that the imagination needed to enact these protocols cannot rely on shared memory, but must be renewed and reworked as contexts change, bringing new ways of understanding and engaging with gender equality.

In our earlier chapters we argued that feminist accounts of women's and gender equality work in the local state refer to two different visions for the delivery of public services. The first of these was a shared project to open spaces for participative development of women's equality that could accommodate and engage with diversity as part of a wider Leftist campaign for extended local democracy. One strategy for achieving this was to harness the coercive power of the local state to impose a prescribed agenda for equality through organisational processes and management practice. This strategy was, and continues to be, attacked on the grounds of 'political correctness', wherein equality advisors are characterised as 'thought police'. On the other hand there were references to forms of awareness raising leading to perceptual shifts, organisational culture change and ownership of equality as a core value. Importantly, many of the changes that seemed like radical coercion in the 1980s are now taken for granted as good management practice.

The successful use of coercive political and management power within the GLC and some Left Labour local authorities in the 1980s was driven by a particular vision of what the experience of delivering and using public service provision should be like. The imaginary dimension that informed and nourished this vision was fragmented, not unitary. It was located in and has lived on in the wealth of independent self-organised, prefigurative campaigning activities and networks in which many local authority workers also participated. While many were sceptical about accepting state funding and loss of independence, for others the local state became a legitimate focus for demanding rights as citizens to a fair share of resources, access to jobs and decision making positions (see Chapters 3 and 4). Moreover, many of the self-organised activities, and processes for representation developed by women's committees and units, were prefigurative in the sense that they set out to create the processes for governance of public services and for an extended local democracy within the local state, which was at odds with the hegemonic political view.

The hegemony fought back and, in the face of massive local government restructuring, central government control of resources and media attacks, the alternative vision for democratic and gender sensitive public service delivery ebbed. During the 1990s and 2000s the business case took hold bringing with it a consumer culture based on individual choice within public services. A market driven equality ethos was developed, one of 'quality service' tailored to individual customers within diverse communities. Our research indicates that, in order to survive in a hostile environment, the utopian vision shifted in some local authorities from one driven by the desire for extended local democracy to one where public services are run on business principles, redefining equality as quality of service for local communities. Neither of these visions addresses unequal power and resistance to the fundamental shift in gender relations that was implied in feminist utopian imaginary and, in this sense, neither are likely to deliver more than limited success. Both visions are fundamentally challenged by neo-liberal administrations currently in power and on the ascendance. Their vision is a neo-liberal meritocracy in which inequality is normalised,[2] gender as a generic category of inequality disappears and in which immigrants, the vulnerable, unemployed and disabled people are increasingly demonised.

Leading up to and following the introduction of the GED in 2006, aspects of a prefigurative view of the state were rekindled briefly. Once again it was possible to glimpse the state as an active agent for promoting fairness and good relations between communities as well as eliminating discrimination. The development of legislation that reframed equality as positive duties on public authorities and moved away from static, individualistic and retrospective legal models felt like the next step in the desired direction of travel. Moreover the requirement for public bodies to consult with interest groups opened up a space for local democracy by encouraging coalitions to form to interrogate how policy decisions would impact on gender relations and to re-imagine what might be possible. Most interestingly, the new legislation made it possible for the coercive power of the state to be used against the state itself because, ultimately, it allows organised equality groups to use the law to challenge the decisions and actions of public authorities. Legislation of this type requires a government that is confident that it can meet the expectations of its citizens and carries some risks (Nonet and Selznick, 1978/2001). The political response to the economic crisis in the UK meant that this was not the case and the window of opportunity began to narrow for reflexive legislation when the leading challenge by the Fawcett Society against the public spending cuts of the newly formed coalition government was defeated. The legislation has, however, had some impact and decisive challenges against the local state in response to subsequent cuts to public services have succeeded.

The partial implementation of the Equality Act 2010 weakened the gains made by the GED by replacing the requirement to draw up strand specific (gender, race and disability) equality action plans with a generic duty which allows public authorities to select a local priority for action that need not cover all strands. Moreover it removed the express requirement to consult before equality plans had been adopted, or priorities decided. In local authorities the move to integrate equality strands anticipated legislation for a single equality duty, and was embraced as an expression of organisational convenience. Generic equality impact assessments could be more easily managed within established organisational processes and structures, where there was little time for reflexivity or dialogue. The removal of centrally defined equality targets was welcomed by some local authorities which found them to be inconsistent with local priorities. The invitation to select priorities would appear to open up opportunities for co-operation with local communities. But without the need for consultation and in the context of severe public spending retrenchment that followed the election of a Conservative-led coalition government, choices are limited. Our research findings confirm the concerns expressed in responses to the PSED review that removal of clear direction to comply with a specific duty for gender will lead to loss not only of transformative gender equality but loss of any gender perspective (Fawcett Society, 2013).

In the context of the unequal impact of austerity, where women are losing jobs and care services, feminist researchers are affirming the economic and social value of women's contribution to society in order to restore the link between social democracy and transformative feminist agendas (Women's Budget Group, 2013). The social value of care and ways of organising care within social relationships were at the core of utopian imagination within feminist writing of the 1970s (see, for example, Le Guin, 1986; Piercy, 1979). Re-stating the case for collective responsibility of care traditionally assigned to women, and how to support and reward carers on a basis of recognition of their vital social and economic contribution, would build on early feminist campaigns for women's legal and financial independence (Women's Liberation Campaign for Legal and Financial Independence, 1975; Rowbotham, 1990, p.149).

In the face of a hostile state, smaller, more 'liberal' outcomes can be appreciated as markers, signalling intent towards the desired direction of travel. They have practical value and meaning for those involved in implementation and those who are the intended beneficiaries. Gender mainstreaming, from this perspective, is a necessarily unfinished project; one that offers potential but opens spaces for activism only wide enough to push at the boundaries of the possible and, in the wrong hands, can be used to dissipate accountability for equality. Similarly equality impact assessments can be valuable tools for thinking reflexively about policy making or, if done mechanistically, can be used simply as a way of justifying poor equality outcomes.

There is a struggle underway to defend gender equality within a redistributive state, against a different vision of gender equality on neo-liberal terms, in which women are invited to participate equally on company boards and the individual is invited to be an actor within an unregulated market. These are not steps in the transformative direction of travel. There is no recognition of the vital economic or social contribution of caring or of domestic labour. In this context equality impact assessments offer an instrument to enforce explicit recording of unequal impact on women of austerity measures, but not to prevent them. The legislation allows for independent organisations to make legal challenges when public authorities do not comply, but in its weakened state following the changes in the Equality Act 2010, only with variable and unpredictable success (Women's Budget Group, 2013).

Our research confirmed the view, established repeatedly by research into the effectiveness of equality legislation, that no change that advances gender, women's or other forms of equality is secure without leadership and activism to breathe life into it and to lobby for improvement when it is inadequate. In a review of the impact of both the specific duties and the PSED, Clayton-Hathway (2013) found, as we did, uneven levels of compliance with legislation in relation to each of the protected characteristics. Submissions to the government review of the PSED were consistent in making specific recommendations for strengthening the PSED, with more explicit guidelines, monitoring and stronger enforcement by public authority leadership. It was evident from this review that the loss of requirement to engage with specific strands left little room for consideration of how protected characteristics might intersect, or of how these intersections might be addressed in practice.

Measures to ensure compliance are therefore a necessary but insufficient framework for advancing equality. Imagination, leadership and activism able to support dialogue across differences are vital to bring life to local democracy. Equality duties that embed genuine and enforceable consultation into decision making in public services provide a unique opportunity to combine compliance with coalitions of activism. Policy becomes a process shaped by actors who find spaces to intervene and to reshape the interpretation and implementation of specific policies within the parameters set by the legislation (Newman, 2002, 2012). Within these spaces, created by requirements to comply with legislation, interpretations of gender equality are contested and, as our research participants demonstrated, there is room for conversation, dialogue and development of more understanding of how to engage with gender equality and with intersectionality in practice (Bacchi and Eveline, 2010; Squires, 2007).

In this context the distinction between transformative and liberal agendas, made by feminist researchers in the first decades of women's equality work in the local state, may be a distraction from the choice we are faced with now. In the context of the neo-liberal dismantling of the redistributive regulatory state, the gradual development of an equalities architecture that requires public bodies to promote equality across its seven distinct strands can now be appreciated as indeed transformative in its potential for opening up spaces for 'forward dreaming', and for a vision of a more equal society to take hold. However, the challenges of how to maintain this momentum remain. The equality duty provides an instrument requiring explicit acknowledgement and mapping of unequal and cumulative impact of austerity measures on different groups of women and of widening inequality. At the same time it provides a call to action, an invitation to re-imagine redistributive justice. It represents an opportunity, however weakened, to consider how we could conceptualise and construct gender equality in order to challenge policy and practice that falls short of our expectations.[3]

Forward dreaming, current challenges to equality work in the local state

There is inevitably a gap between the dream of a new society and its implementation. Any vision requires policy to put it into practice but policy can only be a step in the direction of travel and will therefore always fall short of the dream. The space between the vision and its implementation offers opportunities for activism but also the danger that the direction of travel may be obscured and the policy detached from the dream. This may be particularly likely when the dream needs to be flexible enough to encompass different interests. Our research also indicates that those closest to the implementation are likely to come under pressure to conform to hegemonic perspectives. Activists and leaders therefore need to maintain a constant vigil to ensure that the link between the direction of travel and the vision is maintained.

Feminist researchers have a vital role to play in affirming the specificity and complexity of women's lived experiences of inequality and their strategies of resistance to institutional practices that reproduce inequality. In Chapters 2 and 3 we mapped the territory of critical analyses of the welfare state in relation to gender, race, sexuality, disability and class, and how feminists have attempted to mobilise its coercive power towards emancipation for women. In this final section we draw from our experience as researchers and activists to look beyond our research, towards the future, to signpost specific challenges for sustaining equality practice and opportunities for researcher activist collaborations.

A key challenge that emerged from our research was building a knowledge base that enables practitioners to engage with the complexity of women's lived experience. We need to continue to develop our understanding of how gender equality can be constructed, or undermined, through the policy process (Bacchi and Eveline, 2010). In addition to eliciting data we need to build our capacity for interpreting it. Our research participants referred to lack of internal resources to analyse the data collected through equality monitoring and reliance on expert consultants to conduct complex equality impact assessments. There was little evidence of opportunity for critical discussion of what was being measured or for what purpose. It was evident that the predominant discourse was a neo-liberal conceptualisation of equivalence and entitlement between women and men. Understanding of asymmetrical power relations was limited to individual actors and feminist networks who were, despite the GED, often marginalised from the formation and implementation of policy. Building capacity for strengthening the involvement of stakeholders and improving the quality of gender equality impact assessments was a priority identified by equality advisors in each of our case studies. However, the notion of capacity building and its associations with a vision of incremental learning and change does not address gendered power and resistance or critically interrogate gendered, raced, heterosexist or disablist discourses of welfare. The quality of impact assessments, in our research, was limited both by the capacity and resources available to individuals within the parameters of a predominantly liberal equality discourse and by the nature of their individual commitment to changing gender relations and equality.

As we neared the end of our fieldwork in 2009, the programme of significant austerity measures had already begun, leading to major restructuring of public services and significant reduction in the resources available for equality work. One of the key issues in discussions on the gender impact of austerity budget cuts relates to the loss of expert resources and equality practice that has been built up over time. Reduced funding is leading to the closure of equality networks and independent organisations where this expertise is held. There is a loss of continuity and expertise developed by equality practitioners in local authorities and in inter-organisational networks. We are seeing the stripping away of infrastructure and of resources to support equalities work and increasing reliance on a depleted voluntary and community sector to hold public bodies to account for compliance with weakened equality legislation. In this context researchers have a vital role to play in working alongside activists to record the impact of austerity measures, but also to develop the knowledge base and strategy to engage with change in how public services are organised and governed.

A related issue concerns the nature of the evidence base required by equality legislation to achieve compliance. The requirement in the Equality Act 2010 to collect data on service user groups and employees with protected characteristics would seem to support actions to improve the material reality of women's lives. However, performance measures tied to specific protected characteristics mask the complexity of women's lives and their contested value base, leaving little space for discussion or consultation on how these characteristics might map onto need and how, if necessary, change can be effected. Feminist researchers can offer activists a resource to maintain focus on asymmetrical gender relations and for sustaining effective consultation and critical evaluation of strategies for change. Activist/researcher alliances, such as those resourced by the Women's Budget Group and Fawcett Society in the UK, are already playing a vital role in developing instruments to enable activists, practitioners and researchers to track the cumulative impact of austerity measures on women with additional protected characteristics. These are being taken up by local activists and demonstrate that the PSED, for all its failings, does provide a means to publicly confront and make visible the cost to women of neo-liberalism and of the loss of potential for municipal feminism.

During the period we have researched, the predominant legislative and public sector gender equality discourse has changed from women's equality to gender equality, from equal opportunities, to managing diversity and gender mainstreaming. Social policy and legislative change have constructed equality in terms of as fairness, social inclusion and cohesion, capability and human rights, and now protected characteristics. Local equality practitioners and activists have created instruments for promoting gender equality within the parameters set by each of these discursive shifts, mobilising the discourses available in ways that are pragmatic and skilful within fluid and dynamic political contests. However, the complexity of feminist thinking and practice developed to engage with intersections of inequality and identity and how women experience these is in danger of being lost from view. Equality practice is diminished by a narrowing notion of 'evidence base' in which evidence of inequality is reduced to statistical measures and the embodied experience of everyday institutional sexism is obscured. Feminist research and activism has developed a rich and contested critique of gendered knowledge production and methodological approaches for affirming the value of data based on embodied and lived experience. Feminist researchers have a role to play in promulgating this resource, working alongside activists to develop strategies that can challenge predominant neo-liberal discourses, offering spaces where transformative practice can be developed.

Feminist critiques demonstrate that the state always and necessarily plays a key role in constructing gender relations. The state touches almost every aspect of women's lives through economic and social policy that can reward, punish, regulate, resource, protect or undermine the organisation of reproduction. However, political will is frequently contradictory, leaving potential for working the spaces of power and activism. We have argued that engaging with imagination and prefigurative practice was at the core of the early decades of equality work, which challenged the gendered assumptions within established professional practice and understanding of disadvantage. Our research relating to the later period presents us with a paradox: at the very moment when promoting gender equality became a legal requirement, the prospects of achieving it were diminished. The institutionalisation of gender politics had coincided with the decline of organised feminism and a modernised, business-focused local state had replaced a local democratic vision of social justice. The feminist critique of the state, which exposes and challenges the reproduction of inequality, continues to develop and sustain a dynamic and radical vision of women's and gender equality. The local state continues to be a vital location for feminist struggle, for an evolving vision of participatory local democracy and for the production of public services that are central to a better future for women from all backgrounds. We have argued that the state can support this vision with reflexive legislation that frames equality as a duty rather than an opportunity, but the commitment and political will to do this must be unequivocal.

To limit discussion of the local to the local is no longer tenable as nation states and their welfare services are intermeshed increasingly with devolved and global institutions (Walby, 2000, 2002). Within the UK devolution has impacted on gender equality with the Scottish Parliament and the Welsh Assembly taking more direct and innovative steps to promote and embed it in policy and processes than Westminster (Breitenbach, 2006; Chaney, 2004, 2012; Kenny and MacKay, 2011; Mackay and McAllister, 2012). Chapter 3 highlighted that the implementation of the Public Sector Equality Duty has been particularly affected by devolution and future research is needed to monitor and compare progress in the regions. The institutionalisation of gender equality pertains to local, devolved and nation states but also transnational and global institutions. There are competing visions of gender equality in these institutions, sometimes seemingly embodied in the arrival of women leaders within powerful positions in financial and state organisations, often identified with neo-liberal agendas. Others seek justice for women in the poorest nations of the world (see for example Wilson *et al.*, 2005). Feminist research networks offer a resource for engaging with this complexity and can help to consolidate the revival of feminist activism in a world that is increasingly divided by inequality. The growth of transnational coalition work, stimulated by the decade of UN conferences between 1975 and 1985 has proved effective in relation to specific issues such as violence against women (Basu, 2013; Bunch and Fried, 1996). Protocols developed through feminist and anti-racist activism within bodies such as the UN, the EU and the Council of Europe continue to provide leverage for local use. The scope of issues addressed is wide and strategies reflect the interpenetration of local and global, cyber and material worlds opened up by new technology. In the UK, and internationally, the growth of web based women's and feminist campaigning networks indicates that awareness of gender inequality and the impulse to create a better world underpinned by equality is alive and well, and continues to be a force for change.

Notes

1 Southall Black Sisters successfully used the Race Equality Duty in 2008 to challenge cuts to domestic violence services specific to black and minority ethnic women made by Ealing Borough Council: *R (Kaur) v London Borough of Ealing* [2008] EWHC 2062 (Admin).

2 See for example Theresa May's first equality strategy speech as Minister for Women and equalities:
https://www.gov.uk/government/speeches/theresa-mays-equality-strategy-speech (accessed 24/6/2014).

3 See for example http://www.fawcettsociety.org.uk/wp-content/uploads/2013/07/Red-Tape-Red-Lines-five-reasons-why-government-should-not-drop-its-duty-to-tackle-womens-inequality.pdf (accessed 24/6/2014).

References

Abramovitz, M. (1996) *Regulating the Lives of Women: Social welfare reforms from colonial times to the present*. Cambridge, MA: Southend Press.

Acker, J. (2000) Gendered contradictions in organizational equity. *Organization* 7 (4), pp. 625–32.

Albrecht, L. and Brewer, R. M. (eds) (1990) *Bridges of Power: Women's multicultural alliances*. Philadelphia: New Society Publishers.

Arnup, K. (1989) Mothers just like others: Lesbians, divorce, and child custody in Canada. *Canadian Journal of Women & Law* 3, pp. 18–32.

Audit Commission (2004) *The Journey to Race Equality*. London: Audit Commission.

Bacchi, C. and Eveline, J. (2010) *Mainstreaming Politics: Gendering practices and feminist theory*. Adelaide, Australia: University of Australia Press.

Baden, S. and Goetz, A. (1997) Who needs (sex) when you can have (gender)? 2. *Feminist Review* 56 (Summer), pp. 3–25.

Bammer, A. (1991) *Partial Visions: Feminism and utopianism in the 1970s*. London: Routledge.

Barnes, C. and Mercer, G. (2005) Disability, work, and welfare: Challenging the social exclusion of disabled people. *Work, Employment and Society* 19 (3), pp. 527–45.

Bashevkin, S. (2007) *Tales of Two Cities: Women and municipal restructuring in London and Toronto*. University of British Columbia Press. Also Google ebook (2011).

Basu, A. (2013) Globalization of the local/localization of the global: Mapping transnational women's movements. In C. R. McCann and S. K. Kim (eds) *Feminist Theory Reader: Local and global perspectives*. London: Routledge, 3rd edition, pp. 68–76.

Bell, M. (2010) Judicial enforcement of the duties on public authorities to promote equality. *Public Law* 672.

Benschop, Y. and Verloo, M. (2006) Sisyphus' Sisters: Can gender mainstreaming escape the genderedness of organizations? *Journal of Gender Studies* 15 (1), pp. 19–33.

Bloch, E. (1986) *The Principle of Hope*. London: Basil Blackwell, 3 vols.

Boddy, M. and Fudge, C. (1984) Labour councils and new left alternatives. In M. Boddy and C. Fudge, *Local Socialism, Labour Councils and New Left Alternatives*. London: Macmillan Publishers, pp. 1–21.

Borchorst, A. and Siim, B. (2002) The women friendly welfare states revisited. *Nordic Journal of Women's Studies* 10 (2), pp. 90–98.

Breitenbach, E. (2006) Developments in gender equality policies in Scotland since devolution. *Scottish Affairs* 56 (Summer), pp.10–21.

Breitenbach, E., Brown, A., Mackay, F., and Webb, J. (2002) (eds) *The Changing Politics of Gender Equality in Britain*. Basingstoke and New York: Palgrave.

Bruegel, I. and Kean, H. (1995) The moment of municipal feminism: Gender and class in 1980s local government. *Critical Social Policy*, 44/45, pp. 147–69.

Bristol Women, (1978) 'Nine years together', a history of a women's liberation group. *Spare Rib* 9 (April).

Brooks, D. and Goldberg, S. (2001) Gay and lesbian adoptive and foster care placements: Can they meet the needs of waiting children? *Social Work* 46 (2), pp. 147–57.

Bunch, C. and Fried, S. (1996) Moving women's human rights from margins to center. *Signs* 22 (1) (Autumn), pp. 200–3.

Burgess, G. (2008) Planning and the gender equality duty: Why does gender matter? *People, Place & Policy* on-line, pp. 112–21.

Chaney, P. (2004) The post-devolution equality agenda: The case of the Welsh Assembly's statutory duty to promote equality of opportunity. *Policy & Politics* 32 (1), pp. 63–77.

——(2012) New legislative settings and the application of the participative-democratic model of mainstreaming equality in public policy making: Evidence from the UK's devolution programme. *Policy Studies* 33 (5), pp. 455–76.

Chappell, L. (2002) The Femocrat strategy: Expanding the repertoire of feminist activists. *Parliamentary Affairs* 55, pp. 85–98.

Clarke, J. and Newman, N. (1997) *The Managerial State: Power, politics and ideology in the remaking of social welfare*. London: Sage Publications.

Clayton-Hathway, K. (2013) *The Public Sector Equality Duty: Empirical evidence base*. Oxford Brookes Centre for Diversity Policy Research and Practice.

Cockburn, C. (1977) *The Local State: Management of cities and people*. London: Pluto Press.

——(1989) Equal opportunities: The short and long agendas. *Industrial Relations Journal* 20 (3), pp. 213–25.

——(1991) *In the Way of Women: Men's resistance to sex equality in organizations*. London: Macmillan Education.

——(1998) *The Space Between Us: Negotiating gender and national identities in conflict*. London: Zed Books.

——(1999) Crossing borders: Comparing ways of handling conflictual differences. *Soundings* 12, pp. 94–115.

Coffey, D. and Thornley, C. (2009) *Globalization and Varieties of Capitalism: New Labour, economic policy and the abject state*. Basingstoke and New York: Palgrave Macmillan.

Colgan, F. and Wright, T. (2011) Lesbian, gay and bisexual equality in a modernizing public sector 1997–2010: Opportunities and threats. *Gender, Work & Organization* 18 (5), pp. 548–70.

Combahee River Collective (1983) The Combahee River Collective statement. First published 1977. In B. Smith (ed.) *Home Girls: A black feminist anthology*. New York: Kitchen Table: Women of Colour Press, pp. 272–82.

Commission of the European Communities (1996) *Communication from the Commission: Incorporating equal opportunities for women and men into all community policies and activities*. COM(96)67 final of 21 February.

Conley, H. (2012a) Using equality to challenge austerity: New actors, old problems. *Work, Employment and Society* 26 (2), pp. 353–63.

——(2012b) Economic crisis, austerity and gender equality: The UK case. *European Gender Equality Law Review* 2 (12), pp. 14–19.

——(2013) Trade unions, equal pay and the law. *Economic and Industrial Democracy*, on-line, 10 April.

Conley, H. and Page, M. (2010) The gender equality duty in local government: The prospects for integration. *Industrial Law Journal* 39 (3), pp. 321–25.

Cooper, D. (1993) An engaged state: Sexuality, governance and the potential for change. *Journal of Law and Society* 20 (3), pp. 257–75.

——(1994) A retreat from feminism? British municipal lesbian politics and cross-gender initiatives. *Canadian Journal of Women and the Law* 7, pp. 431–53. See also her web site and new book on *State potential and transformative politics*. Available at: http://www.kent.ac.uk/law/research/beyondkls/statepotential.html

Coote, A. (ed.) (2000) *New Gender Agenda: Why women still want more*. London: IPPR.

Coote, A. and Campbell, B. (1982) *Sweet Freedom: The struggle for women's liberation*. London: Pan Books in association with Basil Blackwell.

Cousins, C. (1999) *Society, Work and Welfare in Europe*. Basingstoke: Macmillan Press.

Coyle, A. (1989) The limits of change: Local government and equal opportunities for women. *Public Administration* 67 (1), pp. 39–50.

Crenshaw, K. (1989) Demarginalising the intersection of race and sex: A black feminist critique of antidiscrimination doctrine. *Feminist Theory and Antiracist Politics*, University of Chicago Legal Forum, 138–67.

Cross, M. (2013) Demonised, impoverished and now forced into isolation: The fate of disabled people under austerity. *Disability and Society* 28 (5), pp. 719–23.

Curno, A. et al. (eds) (1982) *Women in Collective Action*. London: Association of Community Workers in the UK.

Davies, B. and Gannon, S. (2006) *Doing Collective Biography: Investigating the production of subjectivity*. Maidenhead, Berkshire, UK: Open University Press.

Deegan, M. J. and Brooks, N. A. (1985) (eds) *Disability and Women: The double handicap*. Piscataway Township, NJ: Transaction.

Discrimination Law Review (2007) *A Framework for Fairness: Proposals for a single equality bill for Great Britain*. London: Women and Equality Unit.

Edwards, J. (1988) Local government women's committees. *Local Government Studies* (July/August), pp. 39–52.

Eisenstein, H. (1991) *Gender Shock: Practising feminism on two continents*. North Sydney, NSW, Australia: Allen and Unwin.

——(1996) *Inside Agitators: Australian femocrats and the state*. Philadelphia: Temple University Press.

——(2009) *Feminism Seduced: How global elites use women's labour and ideas to exploit the world*. Boulder, CO: Paradigm Publishers.

Eisenstein, Z. (1981) *The Radical Future of Liberal Feminism*. New York: Longman.

Ely, R. and Meyerson, D. E. (2000) Advancing gender equity in organizations: The challenge and importance of maintaining a gender narrative. *Organization* 7 (4), pp. 589–607.

EOC (2006) *Gender Equality Duty Code of Practice England and Wales*. Manchester: Equal Opportunities Commission.

Equalities Review (2007) *Fairness and Freedom: The final report of the equalities review*. London: Cabinet Office.

Equality and Human Rights Commission (2009) *The Equalities Measurement Framework*. Available at: http://www.equalityhumanrights.com/key-projects/equality-measurement-framework/ (accessed 10/12/2013).

Equal Opportunities Review (2002) Race equality work needs to focus on outcomes. *Equal Opportunities Review*, Report 120.

Escott, K. and Whitfield, D. (1995) *The Gender Impact of CCT in Local Government*. Manchester: Equal Opportunities Commission.

Esping-Andersen, G. (1990) *The Three Worlds of Welfare Capitalism*. Cambridge: Polity Press.

——(2009) *The Incomplete Revolution: Adapting to women's new roles*. Cambridge: Polity Press.

Eveline, J. and Bacchi, C. (2005) What are we mainstreaming when we mainstream gender? *International Feminist Journal of Politics* 7 (4), pp 496–512.

Fawcett Society (2012) *The Impact of Austerity on Women*. Available at: http://fawcett-society.org.uk/the-impact-of-austerity-on-women/#sthash.aqdV0d9A.dpbs (accessed 19/6/2014).

——(2013) *The Fawcett Society's Policy Submission to the Review of the Public Sector Equality Duty*. Available at: http://www.fawcettsociety.org.uk/wp-content/uploads/2013/04/Fawett-submission-to-Review-of-the-Public-Sector-Equality-Duty-April-2013.pdf (accessed 1/62013).

Fine, M. and Asch, A. (eds) (1984) *Women with Disabilities: Essays in psychology, culture and politics*. Philadelphia: Temple University Press.

Flannery, K. and Roelofs, S. (1984) Local government women's committees. In Joy Holland (ed.) *Feminist Action I*. London: Battle Axe Books, pp. 69–90.

Fletcher, J. (1998) Relational practice: A feminist reconstruction of work. *Journal of Management Inquiry* 7 (2), pp. 163–86.

Flick, B. (1990) Colonization and decolonization: An aboriginal experience. In S. Watson (ed.) *Playing the State: Australian feminist interventions*. London: Verso, pp. 61–67.

Franzway, S. and Fonow, M. M. (2011) *Making Feminist Politics: Transnational alliances between women and labor*. Champaign: University of Illinois Press.

Fraser, N. (2009) Feminism, capitalism and the cunning of history. *New Left Review* 56, pp. 97–117.

Fraser, N. and Gordon, L. (1994) A genealogy of dependence: Tracing a keyword of the US welfare state. *Signs* 19 (2), pp. 309–36.

Fredman, S. (2001) Equality: A new generation? *Industrial Law Journal* 30 (2), pp. 145–68.

——(2011) The public sector equality duty. *Industrial Law Journal* 40 (4), pp. 405–27.

Friedlander, E. (1996) Introduction. In Eva Friedlander (ed.); Irene M. Santiago (foreword) *Look at the World Through Women's Eyes: Plenary speeches from the NGO forum on women, Beijing '95*. New York: NGO Forum on Women, Beijing '95 Inc., pp. xxi–xxviii.

Friedman, H. and Meredeen, S. (1980) *The Dynamics of Industrial Conflict: Lessons from Ford*. London: Croom Helm.

Gates, G. J., Badgett, M. V. L., Macomber, J. E., Chamber, K. (2007) *Adoption and Foster Care by Gay and Lesbian Parents in the United States*. The Williams Institute, UCLA School of Law, UCLA.

Gelb, J. (1989) *Feminism and Politics: A Comparative Perspective*. Berkeley: University of California Press.

GEO (2011) *Equality Act 2010: The public sector equality duty promoting equality through transparency – Summary of responses to the consultation*. London: Government Equalities Office.

Ginn, J. (2013) Austerity and inequality: Exploring the impact of cuts in the UK by gender and age. *Research on Ageing and Social Policy* 1 (1), pp. 28–53.

Glucksmann, M. (1990) *Women Assemble: Women workers and the new industries in inter-war Britain*. London: Routledge.

Gordon, L. (1994) *Pitied But Not Entitled: Single mothers and the history of welfare, 1890–1935*. New York: Free Press.

Goss, S. (1984) Women's initiatives in local government. In M. Boddy and C. Fudge (eds) *Local Socialism, Labour Councils and New Left Alternatives*. London: Macmillan Publishers, pp. 109–32.

Hancock, A-M. (2004) *The Politics of Disgust: The public identity of the welfare queen*. New York: University Press.

Hantrais, L. (1994) Comparing family policy in Britain, France and Germany. *Journal of Social Policy* 23 (2), pp. 135–60.

Hartman, Y. (2005) In bed with the enemy: Some ideas on the connections between neoliberalism and the welfare state. *Current Sociology* 53 (1), pp. 57–73.

Haug, F., Andersen, S., Bunz-Elfferding, A., Hauser, K., Lang, U., Lauden, M., Ludemann, M., Meir, U., Nemitz, B., Niehoff, E., Prinz, R., Rathzel, N., Scheu, M. and Thomas, C. (eds) (1987) *Female Sexualization: A collective work of memory* (E. Carter trans). London: Verso Press.

Heerah, S. and Berrios, E. (1996) *Beyond Beijing: A documentary on the 1995 UN 4th World Conference and NGO Forum on women*. Frogleap productions. See: www.wmm.com/filmcatalog/makers/fm35.shtml? (accessed 19/6/2014).

Heitlinger, A. (1979) *Women and State Socialism*. London: Palgrave Macmillan.

——(1993) *Women's Equality, Demography, and Public Policies: A comparative perspective*. London: Palgrave Macmillan.

Hemmings, C. (2011) *Why Stories Matter: The Political Grammar of Feminist Theory*. Durham, NC and London: Duke University Press.

Hepple, B. (2011) Enforcing equality law: Two steps forward and two steps backwards for reflexive legislation. *Industrial Law Journal* 40 (4), pp. 315–35.

Hepple, B., Coussey, M. and Choudhury, T. (2000) *Equality: A new framework*. Report of the Independent Review of the Enforcement of UK Anti-Discrimination Legislation Oxford: Hart.

Hernes, H. M. (1987) *Welfare State and Women Power*. Oslo: Norwegian University Press.

——(1988) The welfare state citizenship of Scandinavian women. In K. B. Jones and A. G. Jonasdottir (eds) *The Political Interests of Gender: Developing theory and research with a feminist face*. London: Sage Publications, pp. 187–213.

Hick, S. (2000) 'Good lesbian, bad lesbian … ': Regulating heterosexuality in fostering and adoption assessments. *Child and Family Social Work* 5, pp. 157–68.

——(2005) Lesbian and gay foster care and adoption: A brief UK history. *Adoption and Fostering* 29 (3), pp. 42–56.

Hill Collins, P. (1990) *Black Feminist Thought: Knowledge, consciousness and the politics of empowerment*. London: Routledge.

——(1998) It's all in the family: Intersections of gender, race and nation. *Hypatia* 13 (3), pp. 62–82.

Hobson, B., Lewis, J. and Siim, B. (eds) (2002) *Contested Concepts in Gender and Social Politics*. Cheltenham: Edward Elgar.

hooks, b. (1981) *Ain't I a Woman: Black women and feminism*. Boston, MA: South End Press.

——(1991) *Yearning: Race, gender and cultural politics*. London: Turnaround.

Hochschild, A. R. (1983) *The Managed Heart*. Berkeley: University of California Press.

Itzin, C. and Newman, J. (eds) (1995) *Gender, Culture and Organisational Change*. London and New York: Routledge.

Jenson, J. (1997) Who cares? Gender and welfare regimes. *Social Politics* 4 (2), pp. 182–87.

Jewson, N. and Mason, D. (1986) The theory and practice of equal opportunities policies: Liberal and radical approaches. *The Sociological Review* 34, pp. 307–34.

Johnson, N. (1990) *Reconstructing the Welfare State: A decade of change, 1980–1990.* London: Harvester Wheatsheaf.

Kenny, M. and MacKay, F. (2011) Gender and devolution in Spain and the United Kingdom. *Politics & Gender* 7 (2), pp. 280–86.

Kettle, J. (1998) Local initiatives for working women: Feminism, economics, or both? *Local Government Studies* 24 (4), pp. 64–76.

Kirton, G., Greene, A. M. and Dean, D. (2007) British diversity professionals as change agents: radicals, tempered radicals or liberal reformers? *International Journal of Human Resource Management* 18 (11), pp. 1979–94.

Labour Research Department (1995) Disappearing municipal Equality. *Labour Research* (March), pp. 15–16.

Lawrence, J. (2000) The Indian health service and the sterilization of Native American women. *American Indian Quarterly* 24 (3), pp. 400–419.

Le Guin, U. (1986) *Always Coming Home.* London: Victor Gollancz.

Lenz, I. (2007) Varieties of gender regimes and regulating gender equality at work in the global context. In S. Walby, H. Gottfried, K. Gottschall and M. Osawa (eds) *Gendering the Knowledge Economy: Comparative perspectives.* Basingstoke: Palgrave Macmillan.

Levitas, R. (2013) *Utopia as Method: The imaginary reconstitution of society.* London: Palgrave Macmillan.

Lewis, G. (2002) Categories of exclusion: 'Race', gender and the micro-social in social services departments. In E. Breitenbach, A. Brown, F. Mackay and J. Webb (eds) *The Changing Politics of Gender Equality in Britain.* Basingstoke: Palgrave, pp.143–63.

Lewis, J. (1997) Gender and welfare regimes: Further thoughts. *Social Politics* 4 (2), pp. 160–77.

Lind, A. (2004) Legislating the family: Heterosexist bias in social welfare policy frameworks. *Journal of Sociology and Social Welfare* 31 (4), pp. 21–35.

Lister, R. (1994) She has other duties: Women, citizenship and social security. In S. Baldwin and J. Faklingham (eds) *Social Security and Social Change: New challenges to the Beveridge model.* New York: Harvester Wheatsheaf, pp. 31–44.

——(2nd edition 2003) *Citizenship: Feminist perspectives.* Basingstoke: Palgrave Macmillan.

Livingstone, K. (2011) *You Can't Say That: Memoirs.* London: Faber and Faber.

Local Government Improvement and Development Agency (2009) *The Equality Framework for Local Government.* Available at: http://www. local.gov.uk/equality-frameworks// journal_content/56/10180/3476575/ARTICLE (accessed 19/6/2014).

London Edinburgh Weekend Return Group (1979) *In and Against the State.* London: Pluto Press.

Lovenduski, J. and Randall, V. (1993) *Contemporary Feminist Politics: Women and power in Britain.* Oxford: Oxford University Press.

MacKay, F. and McAllister, L. (2012) Feminising British politics: Six lessons from devolution in Scotland and Wales. *The Political Quarterly* 83 (4), pp. 730–34.

MacKinnon, C. (1989) *Towards a Feminist Theory of the State.* Cambridge, MA: Harvard University Press.

MacLeavy, J. (2011) A 'new politics' of austerity, workfare and gender? The UK coalition government's welfare reform proposals. *Cambridge Journal of Regions, Economy and Society* 4 (3), pp. 355–67.

Maddock, S. (1999) *Challenging Women: Gender, culture and organization.* London: Sage Publications.

Maguire, P. (2001) Uneven ground, feminisms and action research. In P. Reason and H. Bradbury (eds) *Handbook of Action research: Participative inquiry and practice.* London: Sage Publications, pp. 59–69.

Mama, A. (1984) Black women, the economic crisis and the British state. *Feminist Review* 17 (Autumn), pp. 29–32.

Marshall, J. (1999) Living life as inquiry. *Systemic Action Research* 12 (2), pp. 155–71.

Maurice, M. and Sellier, F. (1979) Societal analysis of industrial relations: A comparison between France and West Germany. *British Journal of Industrial Relations* 17 (3), pp. 322–36.

Maynard, M. and Purvis, J. (1994) *Researching Women's Lives from a Feminist Perspective.* London: Taylor & Francis.

McCrudden, C. (2007) Equality legislation and reflexive regulation: A response to the discrimination law review's consultative paper. *Industrial Law Journal* 36 (3), pp. 255–66.

Melby, K., Ravn, A-B. and Carlsson Wetterberg, C. (eds) (2009) *Gender Equality and Welfare Politics in Scandinavia: The limits of political ambition?* Bristol: Polity Press.

Meyerson, D. E. and Scully, M. A. (1995) Tempered radicalism and the politics of ambivalence and change. *Organization Science* 6 (5), pp. 586–99.

Morris, J. (1992) Personal and political: A feminist perspective on researching physical disability. *Disability, Handicap and Society* 7 (2), pp. 157–66.

——(1993) Feminism and disability. *Feminist Review* 43 (Spring), pp. 57–70.

——(1998) Feminism, gender and disability. Paper presented at a seminar in Sydney, Australia: February. Available at: http://disability-studies.leeds.ac.uk/files/library/morris-gender-and-disability.pdf (accessed 2/4/2014).

Mudrick, N. R. (1984) Disabled women and public policies for income support. In M. Fine and A. Asch (eds) *Women with Disabilities: Essays in psychology, culture and politics.* Philadelphia: Temple University Press, pp. 245–68.

Mulholland, M. and Patel, P. (1999) Inclusive movements: Movements for Inclusion. *Soundings* 12, pp. 127–43.

Nentwich, J. C. (2006) Changing gender: The discursive construction of equal opportunities. *Gender, Work and Organization* 13 (6), pp. 491–521.

Newman, J. (1994) The limits of management: Gender and the politics of change. In J. Clarke, A. Cochrane and E. McLaughlin (eds) *Managing Social Policy.* London: Sage Publications, pp. 182–209.

——(1995) Gender and cultural change. In C. Itzin and J. Newman (eds) *Gender, Culture and Organisational Change.* London and New York: Routledge, pp. 11–29.

——(2002) Managerialism, modernisation and marginalisation: Equal opportunities and institutional change. In E. Breitenbach, A. Brown, F. Mackay and J. Webb (eds) *The Changing Politics of Gender Equality in Britain.* Basingstoke and New York: Palgrave, pp. 102–23.

——(2012) *Working the Spaces of Power: Activism, neoliberalism and gendered labour.* London: Bloomsbury Academic.

Newman, J. and Clarke, J. (2009) *Publics, Politics and Power: Remaking the public in public services.* London: Sage Publications.

Newman, J. and Williams, F. (1995) Diversity and change: Gender, welfare and organisational relations. In C. Itzin and J. Newman (eds) *Gender, Culture and Organisational Change.* London and New York: Routledge, pp. 108–26.

Nonet, P. and Selznick, P. (1978/2001) *Law and Society in Transition: Towards responsive law*. New York: Harper.

O'Cinneide, C. (2004) *Taking Equal Opportunities Seriously: The extension of positive duties to promote equality*. London: Equality and Diversity Forum.

O'Connor, J., Orloff, A. S. and Shaver, S. (1999) *States, Markets, Families: Gender, liberalism and social policy in Australia, Canada, Great Britain and the United States*. Cambridge: Cambridge University Press.

Orloff, A. S. (1993) Gender and the social rights of citizenship: The comparative analysis of gender relations and welfare states. *American Sociological Review* 58 (3), pp. 303–28.

——(1996) *Gender and the Welfare State*. Estudio Working Paper. 1996/79.

Osawa, M. (2007) Comparative livelihood security systems from a gender perspective with a focus on Japan. In W. Walby, H. Gottfried, K. Gottschall and M. Osawa (eds) *Gendering the Knowledge Economy: Comparative perspectives*. Basingstoke: Palgrave Macmillan, pp. 81–108.

Page, M. (1997) *Women at Beijing: Coalitions, alliances, networking between UK women NGOs*. London: Community Development Foundation.

——(2003) Leadership and collaboration challenges in not for profit partnerships. *Organisational and Social Dynamics* 3 (2) (Winter), pp. 207–25.

——(2007) *Women at Beijing: Coalitions, alliances, networking between UK women NGOs*. EOC funded research published by Community Development Foundation, UK, March.

Page, M. and Conley, H. (2010) Gender mainstreaming: Between compliance and conviction – the practices of translation. *Gender, Work and Organization International Conference*, 21–23 June, Keele University, Keele, UK.

Page, M. L. (2011) Gender mainstreaming, hidden leadership. *Gender Work and Organisation* 18 (3), pp. 318–30.

Parmar, P. (1982) Introduction to 'A Revolutionary Anger'. In A. Curno et al. (eds) *Women in Collective Action*. London: Association of Community Workers in the UK, pp. 92–93.

Patel, P. (1999) Difficult alliances: Treading the minefield of identity and solidarity politics. *Soundings* 12, pp. 115–26.

Pateman, C. (1988) *The Sexual Contract*. Cambridge: Polity Press.

Payling, D. (2014) Socialist Republic of South Yorkshire: Grassroots activism and left-wing solidarity in 1980s Sheffield. *Twentieth Century History*, pp. 1–26. doi: 10.1093/tcbh/hwu001.

Piercy, M. (1979) *Woman on the Edge of Time*. London: The Woman's Press.

Reagon, B. J. (1983) Coalition politics: Turning the century. In B. Smith (ed.) *Home Girls: A black feminist anthology*. New York: Kitchen Table Press.

Reason, P. and Bradbury, H. (2001) Introduction: Inquiry and participation in search of a world worthy of human aspiration. In P. Reason and H. Bradbury (eds) *The Handbook of Action Research: Participative inquiry and practice*. London: Sage Publications, pp. 1–14.

Rees, T. (1998) *Mainstreaming Equality in the European Union*. London: Routledge.

——(1999) Tinkering, tailoring, transforming: Principles and tools of gender mainstreaming, pp. 27–31 in Conference proceedings *Gender Mainstreaming: A step into the 21st Century*. Athens, 16–18 September. Available at: http://www. coe. int/t/dghl/standardsetting/equality/03themes/gender-mainstreaming/EG-ATH%281999%299_en. pdf (accessed 21/1/2014).

——(2005) Reflections on the uneven development of gender mainstreaming in Europe. *International Feminist Journal of Politics* 7 (4), pp. 555–74.

Roleoffs, S. (1983) GLC women's committee: Democratism or feminism. *London Labour Briefing*, April, p. 18.

Ross, L. (2005) Native women, mean-spirited drugs and punishing policies. *Social Justice* 32 (3), pp. 54–62.

Rowbotham, S. (1990) *The Past is Before Us: Feminism in action since the 1960s.* London: Penguin.

——(2010) *Dreamers of a New Day: Women who invented the twentieth century.* London: Verso.

Rowbotham, S., Segal, L. and Wainwright, H. (2nd edition 1979 / 3rd edition 2013) *Beyond the Fragments: Feminism and the making of socialism.* Pontypool, Wales: The Merlin Press.

Rubery, J. and Rafferty, A. (2013) Women and recession revisited. *Work, Employment and Society* 27 (3), pp. 414–32.

Russo, N. F. and Jansen, M. A. (1984) Women, work and disability: Opportunities and challenges. In M. Fine and A. Asch (eds) *Women with Disabilities: Essays in psychology, culture and politics.* Philadelphia: Temple University Press, pp. 229–44.

Sainsbury, D. (ed.) (1994) *Gendering Welfare States.* London: Sage Publications.

——(1999) *Gender and Welfare State Regimes.* Oxford: Oxford University Press.

Sangster, J. and Luxton, M. (2013) Feminism, co-optation and the problems of amnesia: A response to Nancy Fraser. *Socialist Register 2013: The Question of Strategy* 49, pp. 288–308.

Sawer, M. (1996) *Femocrats and Ecorats: Women's policy machinery in Australia, Canada and New Zealand.* United Nations Research Institute for Social Development, Occasional Paper No.6, Geneva.

Sayce, L. and O'Brien, N. (2004) The future of equality and human rights in Britain: Opportunities and risks for disabled people. *Disability & Society* 19 (6), pp. 663–67.

Sclater, E. (2012) *Older Women's Rights in the United Kingdom, NGO Thematic Shadow Report, June.* OWN Europe and NAWO. Available at: http://www.own-europe.org/UKOlderWomenShadowReport2012.pdf (accessed 21/3/2014).

Scott, M. (2002) Women and local government: Dialogue, deliberation and diversity. In E. Breitenbach, A. Brown, F. Mackay and J. Webb (eds) *The Changing Politics of Gender Equality in Britain.* Basingstoke and New York: Palgrave, pp. 164–77.

Segal, L. (2013) Today, yesterday and tomorrow: Between rebellion and coalition building. In S. Rowbotham, L. Segal and H. Wainwright (eds) *Beyond the Fragments: Feminism and the making of socialism.* Pontypool, Wales: The Merlin Press, 3rd edition, pp. 65–102.

Selznick, P. and Cotterrell, R. (2004) Selznick interviewed: Philip Selznick in conversation with Roger Cotterrell. *Journal of Law and Society* 31 (3), pp. 291–317.

Shapiro, J. (1996) Custody and conduct: How the law fails lesbian and gay parents and their children. *Indiana Law Journal* 71 (3), pp. 624–71.

Siim, B. (1988) Towards a feminist rethinking of the welfare state. In K. B. Jones and A. G. Jonasdottir (eds) *The Political Interests of Gender: Developing theory and research with a feminist face.* London: Sage Publications, pp. 160–86.

Smith, B. (ed.) (1983) *Home Girls: A black feminist anthology.* New York: Kitchen Table Press.

Squires, J. (2005) *Is Mainstreaming Transformative? Theorizing mainstreaming in the context of diversity and deliberation.* Oxford: Project Muse, Oxford University Press.

——(2007) *The New Politics of Gender Equality.* Basingstoke: Palgrave Macmillan.

Stanley, L. (1990) *Feminist Praxis: Research, theory and epistemology in feminist sociology*. London: Routledge.

Teubner, G. (1983) Substantive and reflexive elements in modern law. *Law and Society Review* 17 (2), pp. 239–85.

Thobani, M. (1995) Working for equality in the London borough of Hounslow. In C. Itzin and J. Newman (eds) *Gender, Culture and Organisational Change*. London and New York: Routledge, pp. 152–70.

Thompson, B. (2002) Multiracial feminism: Recasting the chronology of second wave feminism. In C. R. MacCann and S-K. Kim (eds) *Feminist Theory Reader: Local and global perspectives*. London: Routledge, 3rd edition, pp. 56–67.

Thornton Dill, B. T. and Zambrana, R. E. (2009) Critical Thinking about Inequality: An Emerging Lens. In C. R. MacCann and S-K. Kim (eds) *Feminist Theory Reader: Local and Global Perspectives*. London: Routledge, 3rd edition, pp. 176–86.

TUC (2001) Changing times – a TUC guide to work–life balance. Bristol City Council *The Time of Our Lives*, pp. 7–9. Available at: http://www.tuc.org.uk/workplace-issues/case-studies/case-study-%E2%80%93-bristol-city-council (accessed 18/3/14).

Turner, L. J., Danzinger, S. and Seefeldt, K. S. (2006) Failing the transition from welfare to work: Women chronically disconnected from employment and cash welfare. *Social Science Quarterly* 87 (2), pp. 227–49.

United Nations (1995) *Platform for Action and the Beijing Declaration*. New York: UN Department of Public Information.

——(1996) *The Beijing Declaration and the Platform for Action*. New York: UN Department of Public Information.

——(2002) Further actions and initiatives to implement the Beijing Platform for Action. New York: UN Department of Public Information. Available at: http://www.un.org/womenwatch/daw/followup/beijing+5.htm (accessed 19/6/2014).

Veitch, J. (2005) Gender mainstreaming in the UK government. *International Feminist Journal of Politics* 7 (4), pp. 600–6.

Wainwright, H. (2013) Reporting back from conditions not of our choosing. In S. Rowbotham, L. Segal, and H. Wainwright (eds) *Beyond the Fragments: Feminism and the making of socialism*. Pontypool, Wales: The Merlin Press, 3rd edition, pp. 26–64.

Walby, S. (1990) *Theorizing Patriarchy*. Oxford: Blackwell.

——(2000) *Globalization and Inequalities: Complexity and Contested Modernities*. London: Sage Publications.

——(2002) Feminism in a global era. *Economy and Society* 31, pp. 533–57.

——(2005a) Gender mainstreaming: Productive tensions in theory and practice. *Social politics: International Studies in Gender, State and Society* 12 (3), pp. 311–43.

——(2005b) Introduction: Comparative gender mainstreaming in a global era. *International Feminist Journal of Politics* 7 (4), pp. 453–70.

——(2007) Introduction: Theorizing the gendering of the knowledge economy – Comparative approaches. In S. Walby, H. Gottfried, K. Gottschall and M. Osawa (eds) *Gendering the Knowledge Economy: Comparative perspectives*. Basingstoke: Palgrave Macmillan, pp. 3–50.

——(2011) *The Future of Feminism*. Cambridge: Polity Press.

Wanganeen, R. (1990) The aboriginal struggle in the face of terrorism. In S. Watson (ed.) *Playing the State: Australian feminist interventions*. London: Verso, pp. 67–70.

Ward, L. (2000) Learning from the 'Babe' experience: How the finest hour became a fiasco. In A. Coote (ed.) *New Gender Agenda: why women still want more*. London: IPPR, pp. 23–32.

Waring, M. (1988) *If Women Counted: A new feminist economics*. London: Macmillan.

——(1995) *Who's Counting? Marilyn Waring on Sex, Lies and Global Economics*. Terre Nash. Available at: http://www.forum.awid.org/forum12/2013/02/gross-domestic-product-gdp-growth/ (accessed 1/1/2014).

Watson, S. (ed.) (1990) *Playing the State: Australian feminist interventions*. London: Verso.

Webb, J. (1997) The politics of equal opportunity. *Gender, Work and Organisation* 4 (3), pp. 159–70.

——(2001) Gender, work and transitions in the local state. *Work, Employment and Society* 15 (4), pp. 825–44.

Williams, F. (1989) *Social Policy: A critical introduction – Issues of race, gender and Class*. Cambridge: Polity Press.

——(1992) Somewhere over the rainbow: Universality and diversity in social policy. In N. Manning and R. Page (eds) *Social Policy Review 4*. Canterbury: Social Policy Association, pp. 200–219.

——(1999) Good enough principles for welfare. *Journal of Social Policy* 28 (4), pp. 667–87.

Williams-Findlay, R. (2011) Lifting the lid on disabled people against cuts. *Disability and Society* 26 (6), pp. 773–78.

Wilson, A. (1978) *Finding a Voice: Asian women in Britain*. London: Virago.

Wilson, E. (1977) *Women and the Welfare State*. London: Tavistock.

Wilson, S., Sengupta, A. and Evans, K. (2005) *Defending our Dreams: Global feminist voices for a new generation*. London: Zed Books.

Women's Budget Group (2013) *Women vs Local Cuts: Challenging gender equality impact assessments and local government budgets*. Available at: http://www.wbg.org.uk/budget-analysis/english-local-government-budgets/ (accessed 10/12/2013).

Women's Liberation Campaign for Legal and Financial Independence (1975) *Demand for Independence* (Pamphlet), 2nd edition 1990.

Women's National Commission (WNC) (1982) *Background Note*. January.

Wong, L. (1998) *Marginalization and Social Welfare in China*. London: Routledge.

Woodward, A. (2003) European gender mainstreaming: Promises and pitfalls of transformative policy. *Review of Policy Research* 20 (1), pp. 65–88.

——(2004) Building velvet triangles: Gender and informal governance. In Thomas Christiansen and Simona Piattoni (eds) *Informal Governance in the European Union*. Cheltenham: Edward Elgar, pp. 76–93.

Wrench, J. (2005) Diversity management can be bad for you. *Race and Class* 46 (3) (January), pp. 73–84.

Wright, M. (2002) Life after the GLC: Local government and the equalities agenda in England. In E. Breitenbach, A. Brown, F. Mackay and J. Webb (eds) *The Changing Politics of Gender Equality in Britain*. Basingstoke and New York: Palgrave, pp. 178–98.

Yuval Davies, N. (1997) *Gender and Nation*. London and Thousand Oaks, CA: Sage Publications.

Index

inequality: challenging 105; gender 103; and identity 128; lack of understanding 103; pay 43–4; structural measures of 31; women's lived experiences 126
International Women's Week 62–3
intersectionality 87, 91, 98, 105–11, 119–21

Jansen, M. A. 19, 21–2
Jewson, N. 30, 45, 47–8
job evaluation 64
joint commissioning 108, 110

Kean, H. 36–7, 38
Kelly, Ruth 49
knowledge, loss of 87
knowledge base, building 126

labour market: decommodification 12; exclusion 22; the marriage bar 15, 16; participation 12, 15, 18
Labour Party 28, 29, 32–6, 34, 35–6, 37, 38, 40–1, 41, 48, 62, 63, 69
language, politically neutral 87
Lawrence, Doreen 51
Lawrence, Stephen 44, 51, 53n8
leadership 125; collaborative 100–5; feminist 88–95, 100–5; lack of 103; location of 111; political 60, 61, 68, 70–2, 95–100, 112, 114
Leeds 33
Left Labour 32–6, 34, 38, 55, 78, 112, 122–3
level playing field notions 112
Levitas, R. 117–8
Lewisham, London Borough of 32, 39–40
LGBT communities 21, 62–3
liberalism 14
liberating state, the 6, 17–9, 118–9
Lister, R. 17
Livingstone, Ken 52n2
lobbying 44–5, 93, 107, 125
local democracy 61, 65, 71, 72
local government: budgetary pressure 108, 111–2; changing role of 73–4; cross directorate working groups 61; cutbacks 32; democratisation 38, 43–4; departmental accountability 64; desire for change 71; due regard 45; early period activism 32–6; equal opportunities policy 33; equalities budgets 67; Equality Act 2010 48–51; equality benchmarking 43, 44; Equality Impact Assessment (EIA) 45–6, 47, 50;

equality legislation reform 44–8; feminist engagement 121–2; feminist transformational agenda 34; future challenges 126–9; GED implementation 78–115; gender equality business case 41–4; gender equality in 28–52; gender mainstreaming strategy 29–30; implementation gap 47–8; internal redistribution of resources 60–1; international context 52; long and short equality agendas 30–2, 38, 65; modernisation 100; municipal feminism 36–9; outsourcing 89; policy compliance 64–5, 68–70; political leadership 60, 61, 68, 70–2; and power 61–5; practitioner reflections 54–77; privatisation 89; restructuring 42–3, 88–95, 110, 123; socio-economic duty 49; sustaining momentum 72–5; and transnational feminist activism 39–41; utopia building in 121–6; women move into senior management 43–4
Local Government Act 1988, Section 28 35, 44, 62–3
local government support agency 70
local state, feminist struggle and the 5
London Edinburgh Return Group 5
London Edinburgh Weekend Return Group 17, 22
London Fire Brigade 69
London Trades Council, Working Women's Charter 33–4
Lovenduski, J. 23, 33, 36

Maastricht treaty 40
male breadwinner models 6, 15, 16, 19, 19–21
male dominance, challenging 66
managers: perceptual shift 81–2; political commitment 84; risks 82; women 43–4, 103–4
marginality 120
marketisation 5, 19, 42
marriage bar, the 15, 16
Mason, D. 30, 45, 47–8
May, Teresa 50, 129n2
mega events 74
minimum standards quality mark 86
Morris, J. 22
MPs, women 41–2
Mudrick, N. R. 21, 22
multi-agency partnership approach 85–8
municipal feminism 7, 33, 36, 36–9, 43, 61, 80, 114, 120

For Product Safety Concerns and Information please contact our EU
representative GPSR@taylorandfrancis.com
Taylor & Francis Verlag GmbH, Kaufingerstraße 24, 80331 München, Germany

www.ingramcontent.com/pod-product-compliance
Ingram Content Group UK Ltd.
Pitfield, Milton Keynes, MK11 3LW, UK
UKHW020948180425
457613UK00019B/578